# THE NERVOUS HORSE RIDER'S HANDBOOK

## A user friendly guide to building your confidence from within

Emma Cooper

Disclaimer of Liability

This book is designed to provide information and motivation to the readers, and not recommendations. The content is the opinion of the author. Therefore, if the reader wishes to apply the ideas contained in this book, they are taking full responsibility for their choices, actions and results. The author shall have no liability or responsibility to any person, animal or entity with respect to any loss or damage caused directly by the information contained in this book.

Throughout this book, the horse is referred to in the masculine, which represents all horses, regardless of gender, and is used solely for the purpose of consistency.

# CONTENTS

# INTRODUCTION

All riders have times of anxiety, even confident riders sometimes experience nerves and uncertainty. If you suffer from the 'what ifs' when you think about riding your horse, then you are not alone, most people at one time or another will have periods of anxiety and nerves around their horse, and this is nothing to feel ashamed or embarrassed about. If you have got to the stage where you are making excuses not to ride, or you are filled with dread when you think about it; and the time you should be spending enjoying your horse is being affected, then this book is for you. It will give you the tools and techniques to improve your mindset, so you can make the changes that you want to with your confidence. Anyone can learn these skills, and together we will unravel methods for you to achieve your goals.

Riding is not just about training your body and educating your horse; it is just as important to train your mind. Your thoughts, feelings and behaviours are all connected, and you can't change one without the others changing too. Mind training has a crucial part to play in enabling you to reach your dreams and ambitions, even if those dreams are just to be able to enjoy pottering around with your horse; which is just as worthy as aspiring to compete. It's your relationship with your horse, and your own confidence that will give you the most pleasure, whatever your pursuit.

Horse riding can be very emotionally demanding as it involves a relationship between two living creatures, one of which is a large, unpredictable animal, and lack of confidence from one will diminish the confidence of the other.

Often it is not your physical capability that is holding you back, but your state of mind. Even though you may be a capable rider, you might be very self-critical, and full of doubt about yourself, resulting in a blockage in your mind, preventing you from being able to focus while you are riding, and stopping you achieving your goals. Mental training will fill the gap when you reach a point where you don't seem to be able to progress, and feel you have hit a 'wall' in your mind. Often the main problem is with how you are thinking, and your thought patterns. It can be how you view a situation that is often the problem, and not the situation itself. How you think about it affects how you feel, which then in turn can affect how you behave. By changing your thought processes you will change your outlook and actions.

Remember the reason you first wanted to ride, or get your horse, it should be fun, and can be again. You can learn to refocus and change the way you are feeling.

This book is solution based. It doesn't focus on your problems, but in finding solutions to enable you to overcome your obstacles. I share insights gained from many years of successfully helping nervous riders overcome their fears. The information included is what I have found to be most useful in helping these riders.

If something is possible in the world, then it is possible for you to learn too. Throughout this book you will learn the methods and techniques that seem to come naturally to some, because if someone has done it, then you can learn to do it too, it's not mystical, it is all within your reach.

If you always approach your problems in the same way, repeating the same behaviour and responses, then you will always get the same results, preventing you from solving the issues and progressing. You need to approach your problems from another angle, try something new to get different results.

You are about to embark on an exciting journey, where you will explore the link between your mind and your body, and learn how to control your thoughts, and why you should use your feelings to build your confidence. You will be able to understand how your internal programming has an effect on your riding, and how your confidence has an implication on your horse's reactions. By using these straightforward techniques, you will increase your confidence with your horse and build a bond together.

# PREFACE

Having taught many nervous riders over the years, I have found that the majority of them commonly share the same thought processes, and all experience very similar struggles. Finding ways for these riders to move forward and start to enjoy being with their horses again, has been my passion for a long time. Together with the help of my clients, who were willing to explore the training techniques in this book, we found the approaches which really made a difference to them; so I am happy to say, that the methods outlined within, have been tried and tested with success.

I decided to write this book, to share a selection of some of these methods, with the aim to help other rider's who are struggling with confidence issues. With 20 years experience teaching all ages and abilities, my aim is to demystify the secrets which seem to come so naturally to some, and start the reader on a journey of inner confidence.

This guide is more that just writing on a page, I have experienced the chapters in this book, and I hope you will embrace them too. With every rider I teach, I am still learning, and will continue to do so. Each and every rider is inspiring.

*For Mischief, who taught me more than I ever taught him.*

# CHAPTER 1: THE FEAR FACTOR

## Fear

It's completely natural for people to have feelings of fear, which is especially common around horses, and is nothing to be embarrassed about. Fear is intended as a survival response that keeps us alive. We can't completely eradicate our fear responses, but we can train ourselves to adopt a more confident strategy to replace an anxious one. To do this we need to change the way we use our mind and body.

Fear and anxiety are very closely related, and are interchangeable. Our physical and psychological reactions to fear can be sudden, whereas anxiety tends to be chronic. It doesn't matter what we label it, the physical symptoms are the important thing, and how we cope with them to get them under control.

When you ride, nerves and anxiety can come about because you don't want to lose control or get hurt. Firstly, it is important to assess the situation that is causing anxiety, to know whether your fear is justified, and the situation you are in is actually putting you in danger (which is a rational fear, and is there for self preservation and should be listened to), or, if it is something that has escalated in your mind; an irrational fear, talking yourself into all the 'what ifs' of things that you imagine could go wrong; What if I get hurt? Who will look after the kids? What will happen with my job? How will I pay the bills?, and all the worries of modern life today. Often anxiety and fear have simply come about as a result of a break in riding or after having children, and as you get older it is natural to be more cautious. This can be easily overcome by reprogramming your thoughts and controlling your mind in a more positive way.

Some riders have a fear that came from a specific incident such as a fall or accident. In this instance mental recovery should not be rushed, and you should not be put in a situation that you are not happy with until you are ready. By taking small steps at a time, it will ensure that as you regain your confidence, it will be long lasting.

When you are onboard your horse and experience fear and anxiety it can be very unpleasant. You may tense up and become rigid, perch in the saddle and hang on to your horse's mouth through the reins, your heart may race and breathing become shallow, you may feel sick, have a knotted stomach, and can feel pale, sweaty and shaky. Your concentration will also deteriorate making your mind go blank. All these awful side effects are caused by your fear trigger releasing hormones Adrenalin, Noradrenaline and Cortisol, designed to prepare your body for fight or flight; a primeval response from our deep inner instincts. Your horse can sense your fear, as you even give off a smell to him through "pheromones", (a hormone that your body gives off in times of anxiety), and together with your body language, will put him in an anxious state too. Your horse has no idea why you are on edge, and he will conclude that there must be a good reason for it, resulting in every plastic bag, shadow or loud noise being a frightening predator. The cause here is not the external source, such as the plastic bag, dog barking, loud noise etc, but your reaction to it; which results in your horse's behaviour.

Your horse will always be a mirror of your emotions, so if you are tense, how can your horse relax? However, if you start off relaxed and confident, your horse will be much more likely to stay calm. This is why the focus in overcoming your fear needs to be on yourself and not your horse, he is just reacting to you. You need to conquer your fear of getting hurt or out of control, and not the things you have no control over, such as the external sources (wind, dog barking, other people, plastic bags etc), because it is impossible to control all external factors, this is just not realistic.

Horses are naturally nervous creatures because they are prey animals, and in the wild were hunted, and their instinctive reactions of fear and flight are still present. Your horse looks to you for confidence, especially under saddle, in an enclosed space, where he feels more vulnerable. He needs to feed from your confidence. It works the other way too; if your horse becomes anxious and worried, and you react by tensing, then you are telling him he is right to be worried. Tension in you immediately transfers to your horse, causing him to be unable to relax too. This is not a good combination, because horse riding involves two living creatures, lack of confidence from one will diminish the confidence of the other, creating a negative cycle.

Your horse's sensitivity to know when you are anxious should not be under-estimated, similarly when you are confident. You can use this to your advantage by learning to give off a 'confident state' before going near your horse.

It can be hard to focus whilst you are experiencing a 'panic reaction', no matter how many times you tell yourself to relax, it doesn't seem to make any difference. Negative automatic thoughts are mental reflexes which just pop into our heads and block logical thinking. When your brain is in 'stress mode' it cannot properly process the instructions it is being given, let alone act on them. Just telling someone in this situation to 'just get on with it' is not helpful and does not work. This is why you need to be able to practice techniques, so that you are completely prepared, relaxed, and in control of your emotions before you put yourself in difficult situations that have previously caused you anxiety.

When you learn to take control of your emotions and are able to relax, your horse has a much better chance to relax as well. If you start off relaxed and confident, your horse will be much more likely to stay calm, building your confidence back up. This is why horses behave differently for different types of riders, because they mirror the emotions and body language of their rider.

The first steps to relaxing must first come from you, the rider. Your horse, being a prey animal, needs you, 'the herd leader' to tell him there are no monsters to worry about, which will settle him as he will trust you, and give him confidence. Once you have mastered this, your horse will soon relax too, again mirroring your emotions and body language.

## How does your brain process fear?

There is ongoing research into how the brain processes fear. In simplified terms, your fear trigger sends a signal to the brain, which then coordinates your fear response, releasing stress hormones, stimulating the autonomic nervous system, which produces our physical responses (and is why we experience those unpleasant side effects); the relevant negative emotional response in the brain is then processed as a memory.

### Panic Zone/Comfort Zone

Your comfort zone is just that, a comfortable place that has no danger or risk. However, if you want to move forward, challenge yourself, or grow, then you will ultimately have to step outside of your comfort zone. This is where all the excitement happens; new experiences, new challenges and fulfillment.

It is always going to be a bit scary to push yourself forward, or try something new, but it will be exciting too. Staying completely comfortable means not progressing. The thing about your comfort zone is that it will keep stretching and growing, each time you push yourself a little further. What starts off as scary, will soon become normal and boring, so take a deep breath, and plan your next small step. This may be just to tack up your horse and walk him in hand, or take him to the mounting block. There are no rules, only those you make yourself. Each small step can be scary, but imagine how you will feel when you achieve it, and the next time it will be a bit easier.

It can be hard to focus and concentrate whilst you are in a 'panic zone' reaction when riding your horse. When your brain is in 'stress mode' it cannot properly process the instructions it is given. The tools in this book will help you to develop a more positive mindset, without the stress of your horse, so that when you do get on your horse you are completely prepared, confident and relaxed, which will give you both a much better chance of success.

Whenever you address a problem you are experiencing, you are likely to have to move from your comfort zone. This is a process that will see you go through stages, the trick is to move gradually into the 'learning/stretch zone', without tipping into the 'panic zone'. The panic zone is not useful to you, if you slip into this zone you will find it hard to focus and concentrate. We have all experienced this on our horse. For instance, maybe when you were with your instructor; you are riding your horse and for whatever reason start to experience panic, no matter how many times your instructor tells you to relax, or calls out instructions to you, it doesn't seem to make any difference. This is why there is no benefit to working in this mode of stress.

To progress you will need to stretch yourself and move out of your comfort zone, and it is at this point that you may feel that you want to take a step back to an easier time, this is natural, and really signifies that you are about to come out of your comfort zone and into your 'stretch zone', this stage is essential to progressing and just means you are moving forward. Make sure you have support and encouragement, don't feel negative at this point, your journey will be both exciting and scary.

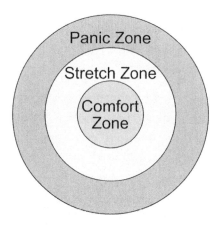

As always with confidence building or a new challenge, you should just take small steps at a time, wait until you are happy and comfortable with that step, until you push to the next step. This will ensure you gain confidence on the way to your goal, and your good experiences will cement the confidence in place.

Use this framework to address each step:

1. Start in your comfort zone

2. Take small steps to your goal, putting you in your stretch zone

3. Repeat until you feel confident

4. You have now increased your comfort zone

5. Now work on your next step

6. Move into your new stretch zone

7. Your comfort zone increases again

8. Next step pushes again into your stretch zone

9. Continue until you reach your goal

If you feel yourself entering your 'panic zone' at any time, then you have pushed a bit too far, stop and look at your process again, and break it down into even smaller steps. This is the method you need to use to succeed, not trying to do too much, too soon. By taking small steps at a time, you will become more skillful, and a by product of this is increased confidence.

As time goes on your comfort zone will grow larger and your panic zone will decrease.

## Never give up

It is so important that you don't give up; you need to keep on trying until you find the key that works for you. If you are not getting the results that you want, then change what you are doing. Because something does not work, it doesn't mean you are a failure, you just need to keep trying, but maybe in a different way, there is no failure, only feedback. An example of this is when a baby is learning to walk, it keeps on trying until it eventually succeeds, no matter how many times it falls down, and how long it takes, it keeps trying, until eventually, it succeeds.

## The importance of the basics

If you can get the fundamentals right, then everything else will fall into place. You must not worry about what other people on the yard think of you and your horse, or what level you are working at.

Don't be afraid to go back to basics. If you develop a secure, balanced position you will feel so much more confident. If your seat is 'plugged in', then you have a direct channel of communication with your horse, which means, that rather than just being a passenger on your horse's back, trying to keep up and trying not to get bounced off, you are engaged, and in rhythm with your horse. You need to imagine you and your horse are one, and when you are 'plugged in', you can communicate to him through your seat.

Without this foundation, you won't be as effective with your aids; for example, if you want to stop or slow down, you may try to communicate this to your horse, but you find yourself perched out of the saddle and hanging on to the reins. Your horse will just pull against this, causing his mouth to deaden, which will make the problem worse in the long term.

Imagine being able to stop on demand. You can easily learn to slow or stop your horse with a half halt; your deeper, restricting seat tells your horse to slow his pace, closing your legs gently around his sides, and closing your fingers on the rein; this is all the communication that should be required.

The reason I focus on stopping, is because, for a lot of anxious riders, this is really crucial to their confidence, knowing that they can stop their horse with ease. I am not saying that just by reading this you will be able to stop immediately; what you need to do is to begin by going back to the correct fundamentals of riding. Step by step you will develop an independent seat and 'feel'.

To you, it may seem that you are sitting in the correct position in the saddle, but in fact you maybe too far in front of the vertical. Your brain will trick you into feeling you are sitting upright, even when you are not. I often find this with riders, and when I show them where they should be, it can feel as though they are really leaning backwards, when if fact, they are upright. You will find that your muscle memory will soon adjust to the 'correct' position.

Find a good instructor to help you. Honestly, you will have more fun focusing on the basics, and establishing those, than trying to rush without feeling secure. You will get lots of unconscious rewards in your mind, as you start to feel you are really riding your horse and are in control. This in itself will really give you a confidence boost. With each small step, you will feel better, and more capable.

The basics are the principles for everything else, once you have these, and an independent, effective riding position, you can go onto do whatever you want; all the disciplines are grounded in good foundations.

It is not only the rider that needs to be well grounded in the basics, riders often encounter problems in their schooling when they are trying to work their horse above his understanding. Your horse needs to have uncomplicated directions from you. Before moving on to a higher level you must be 100% effective at the previous level. For example, if you are moving on to canter, your trot work needs to be balanced and correct, otherwise you will encounter problems, such as your horse running into the transition and becoming unbalanced. This in itself is unsettling for the rider, throwing you off balance too. Both the rider's aids need to be clear and correct, as well as the horse being ready with his training.

A happy relationship between you and your horse is built on trust, communication and understanding of each other, it is a two way process, not you telling your horse, but you listening to his responses, and learning from him as much as he is learning from you. If you over-complicate your instructions, your horse will try to do what he feels you are asking of him. It is rarely the fault of the animal, but the rider that needs to refine their skills.

# CHAPTER 2: THE CONFIDENT MIND

Understanding a little about how your mind works will help you to see how mental training can increase your confidence and your positive outlook.

## The roles of our conscious and unconscious

Your brain is made up of your conscious and unconscious. Your conscious mind is the thoughts you are having right now, the voice inside your head that you can hear; it is critical and is constantly analysing.     It deals with logic, making decisions, and speech.  It can accept or reject ideas, it evaluates situations and people and it takes action.

Your unconscious mind is like a computer that stores all of your experiences and memories, as well as repressed feelings and phobias.   It runs many tasks simultaneously without you being aware of it; all the things you do automatically without thinking, like driving a car, or just walking, talking and breathing.  It supplies knowledge and emotions, and guides your behavioural responses. Like a computer it stores away your experiences, both positive and negative, and these emotions can pop up if you are again put into a similar situation.

You may be surprised to know that your unconscious mind is far greater than your conscious mind (If you picture an iceberg, the vast part of it is unseen, beneath the water; this is a good representation of the conscious mind above the water, and the unconscious mind below). Your unconscious mind has an enormous influence on you in your day to day life, being responsible for your automatic behaviour patterns, which is why you may feel you don't have control over your responses in certain situations, for example, fear.

ICEBERG

Your unconscious mind doesn't know what is fact or fiction, it believes everything you say and imagine, it sees it as the goal and tries to make it come true. This is why people can have phobias about things they have never even done or met. Your unconscious mind deals with your emotions, memories and experiences, your beliefs, imagination and dreaming.

The unconscious mind cannot process negatives. To understand this, take an example; if you are asked not to think of pink elephants, immediately all you can think of is pink elephants. Or if you say don't notice red cars, all you start noticing is red cars!!

This is why the language you use is so important, and why you must state things in the positive. The unconscious mind will translate the statement 'I don't want to be late', into 'I want to be late'. Or 'I won't worry about that' into 'worry about that'. You can see the pattern here. So instead of saying 'I don't know what I am doing', try saying ' I am working on that at the moment to learn what to do'.

So later in the book, when we talk about goal setting, it is imperative that you use positive language to set your goals. Say what you do want, not what you don't want.

## Here is the good part:

It is possible to change your responses and re-train your brain to react in a different way; by creating new thinking patterns, which in turn creates new responses and behaviour patterns. By making these changes, you will allow new neurological pathways to form in your unconscious mind, so your automatic behaviour responses will change. Just by changing your thoughts, your brain will actually create brand new neurological pathways, replacing the old pathways. This is why changing the way you think, really does work, by learning to use positive speech, instead of negative.

To get a clearer picture of how your mind works in this way, we can use an analogy of a ship, like an ancient galleon, with decks hidden below. Imagine your mind as the ship; think of the captain of the ship as your conscious mind, he sits up on the top deck. Every thought you have is a captain's orders, sent down to the crew members below deck. These crew workers below deck are your unconscious mind. They carry out the captains orders no matter what he says and thinks, or whether they are fact or imagined. They cannot see the effect they create, or what is really happening, they just automatically make it happen from below.

So when the captains orders (your conscious thoughts) are negative, for example, "I'll never be able to cope with my horse if he is a bit lively", or "I'm terrified if my horse spooks I will come off", your workers below deck (your unconscious mind), just carry out the orders regardless, and bring up negative feelings to match what is being said or thought, making you feel tense, worried, nauseous and filled with dread. Any good feelings you had are blocked out, and you can only focus on the negatives.

If you have had a bad experience on your horse, the next time you ride, your unconscious mind may bring back the negative thoughts, feelings and behaviour associated with that experience, as it has made a connection between the act of horse riding and the negative experience. This is also true of any bad experience you have had in other areas of your life, not just with horses.

To change this pattern, you need to change your conscious thoughts and internal dialogue into positives, so that your unconscious mind will then search for positive feelings instead of negative ones. To succeed, both parts of your mind need to work together, you can guide your unconscious to work on ideas and solutions to problems that your conscious mind thinks.

## Beliefs

Every person has their own internal reality and belief system that they build up from individual experiences throughout their life. We use our own individual internal filters to interpret things. Often, our representation of things, patterns, people, places and experiences are not the same as the real thing. This is because as we process information we distort, delete and generalise things, so we do not get an accurate picture, and is why different people will each have different perceptions of the same thing; as everyone interprets things differently. The world is the same, we choose how we interact with it, whether we make problems or we have positive, enriching experiences.

Beliefs drive our behaviour and identity. We create our beliefs through our own life experiences, also the repetition of certain thought patterns can become beliefs over time, this is the same whether they are negative or positive. Naturally, our core beliefs have emotions attached to them, and this is why we feel so strongly about them. You may have heard the saying 'Your outer world is a reflection of your inner world', and this is definitely true.

It is important to understand how beliefs are formed, as unhelpful beliefs can be created in your mind from negative experiences you have had, and that have got out of control. To you, this belief becomes a reality, but that does not mean that it is a fact. Beliefs are often created from experiences, not facts. A belief can easily be made stronger by repetitions that are strengthened in your mind, causing a connection to be formed between your trigger and the feelings associated with it. These beliefs become ingrained in us, and they tend to guide us in our everyday lives. Included in these beliefs is our level of confidence and how we define our abilities. We often live within these constraints, believing that is our potential.

## Limiting beliefs

These belief systems are very relevant to your confidence around your horse. You don't need to have had a bad accident or a fall to experience anxiety about riding. Sometimes these feelings can just creep up on you, but that doesn't make them any less real. When you create limiting beliefs about your capabilities as a rider, it doesn't take long before your body believes them, and they spiral out of control, until you find yourself making excuses not to ride. After a negative riding experience, your mind can create limiting beliefs about yourself as a rider. These beliefs have emotions such as fear and anxiety attached to them that influence your behaviour. A downward spiral of negative emotions can quickly grow and you find yourself becoming less and less confident.

Your unconscious mind represses negative memories and the emotions that went with them. They are tucked away, but they will resurface when a stimulus requires them. For example, old memories of feeling like a failure and not confident in certain situations. You push these feelings down inside, but the next time you are put in that situation, your unconscious mind will find those emotions and remind you again how it made you feel.

## How your beliefs affect situations and how to challenge them

Your thoughts result from your feelings and beliefs that you have about particular events. You act on how you feel, which is why people react to the same stimuli in different ways, because their beliefs and thoughts about the event lead to different consequences.

Your thoughts become reality. So you can learn to alter your thoughts to match what you want to see in the outside world.

In everyday life, you often don't pay attention to your beliefs, or your perceptions around events, just accepting that this is how you feel. You should examine your thoughts and feelings about an event if it is causing you anxiety and distress, so you can gain a better insight to why you feel this way. Often it is your own internal beliefs that created the external event, these thoughts triggering a cycle of negative patterns.

Step back and rationalise these thoughts. Your mind has the power here. You can feed yourself more positive information so that your brain works for you, instead of against you.

Instead of trying to change the emotion attached to the event, change your thoughts about the event, this will allow you to experience new emotions when the event happens again. It is the thoughts that trigger the emotion, not the other way around.

Your mind controls your perception of reality, so to have a more positive reality, you must adjust your belief system.

The way to change your reaction to an event, is to change your beliefs and thoughts about it first, in order to feel different emotions.

For example:

Think of an event that you do not have a positive outlook on at the moment. Be honest about how this makes you feel at the moment, be completely honest and write down your thoughts and feelings. Describe the emotion you felt and your behaviours because of them. Describe in detail the situation that has made you feel like this. Describe your thoughts and beliefs about it.

Now examine those beliefs. Write down each belief and ask yourself logically if these beliefs really make sense. Do they help you achieve the emotion you would like?
Now challenge your beliefs. Ask yourself: Are my beliefs logical? Are they based on fact? Are they useful?
It may be that some of your beliefs are useful and rational, while others are not, this is fine. Some maybe based on rational things, whilst some beliefs may be 'what ifs', which can be endless and not helpful.
Identify the bad beliefs that you are having and find three good beliefs to replace each one with, turning the negatives into positives. These beliefs need to be logical, helpful and based on fact.

Now examine how you would feel in the situation with these new beliefs. Do they bring up more positive emotions? If they do, then you need to train yourself to think of these new beliefs every time you think of the event. Over time, with practice, these new positive emotions will give you a more positive perspective.

As you practice more, you will find that you start to challenge your beliefs about situations and events all the time, and it will become easier to change them to positives based on fact.

The way your mind works, the old negative emotions will not be brought up to the surface, and you will find that more positive emotions replace them. You will gradually undo the old negative beliefs, creating a more positive outlook. Eventually this will be automatic, just as previously your negative emotions were automatic.

Make the effort and persevere, and you will notice the difference. Start now, you have nothing to lose and everything to gain. Think of your mental training in the same way as you do your physical training. You need to put the time and effort in to see results. A year from now you will wish you had started today!

## Your model of the world and how this develops

You create your own reality. Your personal perception of the world is your reality. (This is why different people have very different experiences of the same thing). Every person has their own model they build up from individual experiences.

As I referred to previously with beliefs, your representation of things, patterns, people, places and experiences is not the same as the real thing.

The world is the same, you choose how you interact with it; whether you make problems, or you have positive, enriching experiences. Every person's reality is their own. You use your own individual internal filters to interpret things. How you perceive yourself in your head is not a true representation of who you are. The inner doubting voice is just that, it is inside your head. It is easy to change your outlook, reality can be whatever you want it to be.

Repetition is what works with your unconscious mind. Your unconscious will automatically find evidence and emotions to back up what you are telling it and bring these emotions into your conscious, therefore making it seem a lot more real to you.

Try this exercise:

1.  Take a situation or event that is bothering you and causing you negativity and dread.

2.  Now imagine how you would like to feel in this situation.

3.  Change your internal dialogue (basically talking to yourself inside your head, or aloud if you find it easier). Use positive language and say how you would like to feel as a reality. For example, you might say. "I am really looking forward to .......... I know I will enjoy it and it will be exciting. It is natural to be a little apprehensive, and I accept this and know that I will be a success/I will enjoy the experience"

4.  Repetition is needed to allow your unconscious to find the emotions and evidence to back this up.

5.  Continue with this inner positive self talk every day.

6.  You will gradually start to feel different when thinking about the event/situation.

7.  At first you may hear your negative mind, but you just need to stop immediately (even by saying STOP out loud), then replace the language with your new positive phrases. Your unconscious will soon pick up the new habit.

## Thoughts, feelings and behaviour

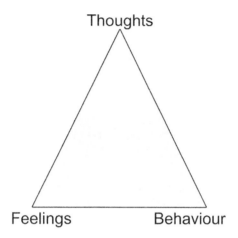

Our thoughts, feelings and behaviours are all connected. When we think about something, we trigger certain feelings, they can be positive or negative. It is these feelings that lead us to exhibit how we behave in these situations.

Because we can learn to control our thoughts, we can then determine how they make us feel, and in turn, change the way we behave in any given situation that arises.

Through learning how your mind works, you will have the tools to be able to change how you think about situations, which will change how you feel, and you will then see a change in how you behave. Situations that have previously caused you stress and fear, will be possible and enjoyable.

# CHAPTER 3: GOAL SETTING FOR SUCCESS

**Where to start?**

To know where to start, you need to know where you are at the moment. To find this out, you can ask yourself some simple questions; there are a few examples below to get you started. You can expand on these depending on your individual situation (it is important that you are honest with yourself when you answer them):

1. Do you ride your horse at the moment, and if so, how often?

2. How do you view yourself as a rider?

3. What are the problems you are experiencing and when/where do they occur?

4. What are the issues you would like to address?

5. Describe the feelings you have that are causing you a problem.

6. Is there a particular incident that you can think of that may have triggered your responses?

7. Why do you want to become more confident?

8. Do you have any medical conditions that should be taken into consideration with your journey?

**Goal setting**

It is vital for success to have a defined goal, as progress can wander off course without having a specific outcome in place, and headway can be slow and vague with no real direction. Setting yourself measurable goals and objectives will help you define exactly what you want, and serve as a plan for how you will get there. Remember to create timelines for achieving each milestone, as this will help keep you focused and on track.

So the first thing to do is to define your goal. Remember, there is no success without planning.

Take your time to investigate thoroughly what it is that you really want, and what success may look like to you. Investing some time at this stage is crucial, don't become impatient, it's important that you are thorough. This can be a challenging process, but is all part of your growth and development into a happier person. Your goals are personal to you, there is no right or wrong, this is about you and your horse being happy and safe together. Don't feel like you need to aspire to be an olympic rider because you are writing down where you want to be.

**Method**

When determining your goal, it is important to use detailed scrutiny, to ensure that what you think you desire, is in fact, what you actually want. Often when we examine what we think we would like to strive for, we find that the result we actually would like, looks a little different.

Start by asking yourself some questions, and then go through and list the advantages, disadvantages, potential opportunities and restrictions of your goal.

1. What is it that you think you want?

2. Why do you think you want this?

3. What is your expectation of this goal?

4. Do you really need what you think you want from the goal, and is the goal the right place to gain this?

5. Where else could you get your desired outcome?

6. Compare methods of attaining your goal?

7. Will you need to obtain any resources?

## Checking validity

Checking the validity of a goal means checking that the goal is well grounded.

The goal must be what you really want, and not what you think you should strive for because of outside influences or pressure from other people.

Work through the reasons for wanting the desired outcome. This is very important to ensure it is what you really want.

## Your outcome - Fine tuning your goal

**Specific** - Be specific about what you want, vague goals are not helpful. Break it down into a specific target; ask who, when, what, where and how. Be positive when defining what it is that you want, always state your goal in positive terms. Use sensory based language to describe the outcome; use all your senses to describe how you will feel when you achieve your goal. If you don't clearly define the goal you will have no clear direction. The more specific the goal, the higher the chance of success, as you can build a clear picture of how to get there. Visualise your outcome, use all your senses and imagine what it will feel like having attained your goal. This will really help to cement a positive outlook and give you something real to focus on through your journey.

**Measurable** - Define a way to measure your goal, so you know when you get there, or how near or far you are away from it, this way you can measure your progress. How will you know when you have achieved your outcome? What will it look like when you get there? How will you feel when you have achieved your goal? It is important to know when you have arrived.

**Achievable** - Make sure your goal is not impossible for you to achieve. It must be within possibility, or you are setting yourself up to fail. Ensure the outcome is one you are able to achieve, and is not 'outside of your control'. When you think about what you want, you need it to be within your power to achieve it. If you choose a goal that is not within your own power to achieve, that is, that you are reliant on outside factors or people to reach the goal, then you are not controlling your own path, so you cannot control your success, and it will be more difficult to succeed. Your goal must not be reliant on other people, it needs to be self initiated, that is, to be able to be started by you alone, not relying on others for your outcome. Changing other people is out of our control.

**Realistic** - Make sure your goal is not an unrealistic 'dream'. The goal must be realistic in terms of where you are; a 'dream' is simply that, and can lead to disappointment. It is good to have dreams, but your goal must be realistic to you. Obviously it is easy to say 'I want to be rich' or 'I want to be famous'. Generally these are not particularly helpful statements. Whilst it is good to be positive and have dreams, these examples are not realistic. It would be better to say 'I would like to have enough money to be comfortable and able to afford the luxuries I want to enjoy my life', and 'I would like to be recognised as being a success at what I do'. A goal does not have to be something you are already capable of, because you can use extra resources to develop yourself and learn new skills. This is ambition, and is realistic.

**Time-bound** - There needs to be time restraints on reaching your goal. If completion of the goal is not set to a timescale, it is likely to keep slipping further into the future. It cannot be open ended. The time frame may change along the way, and it is good to have flexibility, but there must be a clear time frame to reach your goal. (It is fine for it to take longer, this is just how life is sometimes, but no clear timelines will mean you never really have motivation to get started or push yourself forward).

## Step ladder

Make a step ladder to reach your goal. The bottom is where you are now and the top is where you would like to be. Identify ways to get to your goal by breaking the process down into small steps, each step is marked on the stepladder, so you have markers along the way. By having a step ladder to your goal, it makes it easier to achieve each step, giving you confidence that it is within your reach to work your way up the ladder.

## Chunking

This is essential, so you don't feel overwhelmed. Break down your goal into manageable chunks, like stepping stones, so you have a set plan to follow. This method also ensures you have regular rewards and 'highs', so you get a 'buzz' when you succeed to each step, which increases your confidence and spurs you on to continue.

## Progress

Working towards your goal can be stressful at times, it is important to evaluate how you are feeling, you will get to a point where you are moving out of your comfort zone. At this point you may feel that you want to take a step back to an easier time, this is natural, and really signifies that you are about to stretch yourself, this stage is essential to progressing, and just means you are moving forward. Make sure you have support and encouragement around you, do not feel negative at this point. Your journey will be both exciting and scary.

If you hit any hurdles, don't worry, it could be you just need a little more time, if you get to a stage where you feel you are stuck, then these setbacks can be addressed by finding alternative methods to the next step. This is not failure, it is just finding what works for you, and is part of the journey.

Although you will have times of anxiety, you will also have great feelings of achievement as you reach each step towards your goal.

## Flexibility

Although you have made a clear plan to reach you goal, it is important to remain flexible, by nature, things continually change and are fluid; it is important that you accept that your goal can be altered and is not set in stone. If something is not working then it is fine to try a different approach, this should not be viewed as failure, but useful feedback, as is often necessary to progression. Do not be put off if things don't go exactly as you planned. As you work towards your goal, you may find that you change along the way, and grow as a person, therefore, your journey may need to change direction to reflect your new feelings, this is absolutely fine and must not be viewed as negative. You may even change your mind about what outcome you actually want, this is also fine, as we grow we often change along the way.

# CHAPTER 4: BUILDING INNER CONFIDENCE

## Confidence

Our self confidence comes from a variety of factors including our upbringing, parents, experiences at school and during adolescence. As we grow, we develop belief systems which dictate how we feel about ourselves and the world, and govern our everyday lives. Often our beliefs have no basis in reality at all.

It is important to take on board that confidence can be learned and practiced by anyone. You may have said to yourself 'Others seem to be so naturally confident, I am just not a confident person'. This is not a true belief, anyone can become more confident. There are simple steps you can take now to help increase your confidence, and there are things you can do in your everyday life to encourage you to become more confident.

It is only natural that our confidence can be influenced by other people, whether this is good input or negative input. For this reason you should try to be around people who enrich your confidence; it is not healthy to be around people who make you feel bad, distance yourself from the negatives which are in your life. Negatively from other people will destroy your self confidence and will affect all aspects of your life.

The language and words you use can make an incredible difference to how you feel; use positive language, speak confidently to yourself and be kind. Positiveness is contagious, try it and you will see.

Remember that it is how you choose to respond to any situation that dictates how you will feel about it. You have the control. You can develop a positive outlook in everything you do, in all aspects of your life.

## Positive thoughts

You can choose to be positive. You can train yourself to think more positively by concentrating your thoughts on what you can do, and not on what you can't. Every day, think of things you have achieved in your life, and think of the qualities and skills you possess. If you only tell yourself what you can't do, you give yourself no chance to improve, you are only thinking of failure. Positive thinking will give you more energy, more drive and more enthusiasm. Focus on solutions, not problems, and all you need to help you will become clearer. When you have control over your thoughts, you really do gain control over your life.

We know the unconscious mind creates the emotions to match what the conscious mind is telling it, so we can change our internal dialogue into positive self talk, forcing our unconscious mind to create positive emotions.

## Inner dialogue

We all have an inner voice inside our heads that is constantly chatting away in the background, this is our inner dialogue, which can be negative or positive. You may not realise what an impact this has on how you are feeling at any time, but those little negative comments in the background will be contributing to building your stress and anxiety levels; they guide your reactions and how you frame different situations you are in. These negative messages fuel our feelings, and can spiral out of control. We listen to ourselves and believe our statements to be fact, but following these 'apparent' facts make us feel bad. Our minds do not distinguish between what is real and what is imagined, so if you have a negative internal dialogue, your unconscious mind will create the emotions to fit.

To change this cycle, you need to promote a more positive outlook. By changing your internal dialogue to positive you can substantially improve your outlook and happiness, it is just as simple to tell yourself positive things; when you believe and follow them, you will feel better. You can learn how to override the negatives, and replace your internal dialogue with positive truths. Using your mind in this way is just practice.

Because our unconscious mind cannot distinguish between what is real and what is imagined, we can use this to our advantage. There really is 'power in positive thought', we can change our internal dialogue into positive self talk, therefore forcing our unconscious mind to create positive emotions and feelings.

What we believe about ourselves comes across in our attitude, which others reflect back to us, and reinforces our beliefs about ourselves. It also influences how we will perform, if we act confident, we will more than likely be successful. This reinforces positive beliefs and affects our inner dialogue. It is said that your outer world is a merciless reflection of your inner world, so change your inner world if you want your outer world to change.

Self-talk is something we all do naturally all the time we are awake. For some of us this internal dialogue is positive, but for others, a bit of conscious effort is needed to break away from the negative pattern of self-talk. With practice, you can easily turn the tide on these bad thoughts, so that good thoughts replace them and become natural.

So you need to find a way of changing your negative internal dialogue into positive internal dialogue. You can choose to be positive. To start, monitor your thoughts at the moment. Listen to what your inner voice says to you. Is it supportive, or critical? Write down any persistent negative thoughts that you keep getting, then turn these around into positive statements, using present tense, which makes it real, and in the now. Having positive self talk prevents negative internal dialogue from entering your conscious thinking.

Using self talk is a valuable tool when riding your horse. It will help you to focus and shut out distractions. Self talk can be used to concentrate on essential points, and enable you to transform your skills into actions. Develop short phrases to use when you are riding, to refocus and stay positive.

## Thought stopping

Thought stopping is a process used to stop negative thought patterns running around your head. You have the power to control what you can change, and how you react to different situations. Focusing on the things you can change, and not things which are out of your control, is the key to moving positively forward.

Every time a negative thought enters your head, you say "stop", don't let it go any further. Now you use a positive thought and phrase which you immediately say. This crushes the negative, immediately replacing it with a positive, before the unconscious mind has a chance to receive it and start matching the negative emotions. Now the message the unconscious mind receives is positive, so it searches for feelings to match. As with anything else, repetition is key to cementing the changes in place. Don't give up, keep practicing.

## Here is how it works:

Before you start, you need to think about some positive things about yourself, it helps if it relates to the situation you have around your negative thoughts, but it can really be positives about any situation that you have had experience of. Write down some positive phrases and beliefs about yourself that relate to you personally, which you can use to change your internal dialogue in the thought stopping exercise.

As you notice yourself saying something negative in your mind, you can stop your thought mid stream by saying "STOP", or by visualising a large RED BUTTON or a STOP SIGN. There are many variations on this, some people use a big DELETE BUTTON, this is really your choice as to what you choose; some people find it easier to picture something in their mind, while others prefer an auditory cue. Saying "STOP" aloud is really powerful, and having to say it out loud will make you more aware of how many times you are stopping negative thoughts, and where. (You can gradually take this down to a whisper, and then just a thought, once it is ingrained as your automatic response). Then you need to immediately replace the negative thought with a positive belief, using your new positive beliefs and phrases you have written down, so immediatley after saying 'STOP' or visualising your 'RED BUTTON' etc., replace the negative thought with one of these positive beliefs about yourself.

Here is an example:

*I was working with a lady recently who hadn't ridden for a while due to personal circumstances. Through this enforced break in her riding she had talked herself into being anxious of getting on her horse again. She had so much negative dialogue going around in her head, she had forgotten the pleasure that she used to get from riding her horse. She had imagined all sorts of things that could go wrong, which were not based on her 'actual riding ability' and were not facts.*

*We had to change this pattern of how she was reacting each time she thought about riding. So I got her to think back to times when she was confident, and had good riding experiences. (Any positive experiences will work just as well, it is the emotion associated that is important, not the situation). We wrote a script of positive dialogue that personally related to her.*

*Each time she was aware of a negative thought, she STOPPED it in its tracks and replaced it with one of her chosen positive phrases. This reprogrammed her mind to stop focusing on the negatives, and her unconscious started to work on creating positive associations, finding positive feelings from past experiences, and bringing forward the feelings of being capable and confident. By changing her internal dialogue to positive, her feelings started to change into positive ones towards riding her horse.*

## Positive affirmations

You can use positive affirmations to prevent negative dialogue from entering your conscious thinking. To achieve a positive state of mind you need to be able to control your inner voice. Make up some positive phrases that relate to you, try to make them as personal to you as possible so you will believe in them. The purpose of these positive affirmations is to prevent negative internal dialogue from getting into your consciousness, and to break the cycle of negativity. You can achieve exactly what you believe you can achieve, so replace self limiting thoughts and beliefs, such as "I can't" with "I will" and "I can". This positive self talk will help you to create a great sense of momentum. Remember what you have learned; 'when you have control over your thoughts, you have control over your life' and this really is true, happy thoughts fill your life with more happiness.

Good affirmations should be kept short and easy, for example:

"I will feel more confident each and everyday."
"Every small success proves to me that I can do it".
"I am becoming more and more aware of my qualities and skills."

Write some down that are personal to you.

# CHAPTER 5:
# VISUALISATION

## What is visualisation

Visualisation, also known as mental rehearsal, is a technique where you imagine
yourself in a specific environment, or performing a specific activity successfully. It
has been studied by sports psychologists
for many years. Rider's using visualisation
techniques improve their performance
over riders who just use physical training,
and time spent visualising may be almost as
beneficial as time spent in the saddle. This
may be because when you visualise you are

always practicing correctly. It is also a powerful tool to change
old negative patterns into new positive ones, improving confidence, focus and concentration.

Scientific studies have found that the muscles and the unconscious mind cannot distinguish between visualised activity and
actual activity. Our mind and body are intimately connected and
what changes one has an effect on the other. You create what you
imagine. This means that, through visualisation practice, you can
train yourself to react in the correct way automatically, enabling
you to override your 'panic reaction'. This method is very effective; the more you practice, the easier you will find it.

Using visualisation skills can help to relax and reduce tension, sharpen your focus and improve concentration, plus it can control your emotions at times when you really need to refocus and calm your mind. For increasing confidence, it is a great tool for picturing yourself in a more positive state, and can be used for seeing yourself as you would like to be. It's great for all different situations, from learning your dressage test, alleviating competition nerves, improving your general riding skills to practicing being confident around your horse.

We use the same neurological pathways to represent imagined experience as we do if we experience it for real. Thoughts have direct physical effects; mind and body are one system. An example of this is to imagine eating your favourite food, the food may be imaginary, but the salivation is not. Try imagining a crisp fresh apple, you can almost taste it, or imagine placing a yellow, sour lemon on your tongue, this too can make you salivate.

## Visualisation and riding

If you practice visualisation regularly you will find that when you get back in the saddle, your reactions will be exactly as you pictured them. Visualisation is a really good tool for horse riders, because nerves, muscles and ligaments react the same way as they would during the real thing, only subtly.

To use the technique successfully you need to fully immerse yourself into your images, as though you are watching a video of yourself in your mind. You need to use all your senses, the more you can make it real in your mind, feel the emotions, and really focus on your outcome, the more successful you will be. You should see yourself enjoying the activity and feeling happy with your performance. You need to immerse yourself fully into the image with all your senses; sights, sounds, feel, touch and smell. The more you practice, the easier you will find it, the technique is very successful.

## Using modelling for visualisation

Modelling is a great tool, if something is possible in the world, then it is possible for you to learn too. You can model successful people, learn the skills that they use and mirror them for your own success.

It's not rocket science, if someone has done it, then you can learn to do it too. Modelling is a technique used by many businesses. Find people doing what you would like to do and model them, then you too can achieve the successes they have. It is not mystical, it is all within our reach.

Modelling and visualisation can compliment each other, it can give you a focus, especially if you are finding something hard to picture in your imagination. For example, you could watch a video of a rider you look up to, and put yourself in their place in your visualisation. You need to break down what each part of your body will be doing so you can really feel the difference, this will tell your muscles the new position.

## How to do it

Make sure you are in a comfortable place, free of distractions. Plan out what you would like to visualise first. Writing it out is a good idea, as it really makes it real. Once you have got your plan completed, you can start your visualisation in practice.

Visualisation works very well when combined with the relaxation process of self hypnosis, which you will learn about in the next chapter. This is because your mind is in 'Alpha State' and is at it's most receptive to suggestion.

Ride an exercise in your mind including every detail. To start the process you would break a movement down into all of its parts; for example a canter transition; there is a lot to do to set this up, but in reality it happens in a brief moment. You could not possibly think about everything you need to do to ask for canter at the time of the transition; so you can go through it step by step, then once you have it pictured correctly in your mind, you can shorten the sequence to something that will prompt you at the time of riding the transition. The sequence you say must not be longer that the movement, or you will not be able to say the prompts out loud (or inside your head) as you perform the movement. Prepare yourself thoroughly by saying out loud (or you can write this down if you prefer) what you will be doing, and what your horse will be doing in response. The more detail you include, the more success you will have. Use all your senses; the sounds, smells, sight, touch and feelings. Imagine it as your own short film. As you have practiced it perfectly in your mind, your muscles will remember and you have a much better chance of success. After you have got the hang of this at home without your horse, you then need to learn how to apply your mental imagery skills on your horse.

Once back in the saddle say the prompts out loud as you ride the movement. You should be replaying the movement from your visualisation in your mind, therefore it should go as planned. Don't worry if it takes a few goes to get there, just keep practicing. Once you have ridden it correctly, take a moment to stop and capture the feelings, and run through it in your mind again with the new feelings; if you have an instructor present, talk it through with them. (A good instructor will encourage you to have a full understanding of each movement, correct aids and processes, and will answer all of your questions). Remember, what you visualise is what you get! Run through it in your mind like a short film. This way, next time you will recall it even easier.

Get into the habit when you are riding, before you execute a movement, for example, a canter transition, to first picture it as perfectly as you can, see, feel and talk through the transition as you want it to go.

## How visualisation can help with competing

Visualisation can be useful for moving out of your comfort zone, such as when competing, or just progressing towards your goals, which can cause you anxiety. Fear and anxiety can go hand in hand with progress, as you stretch yourself with new experiences. It is how you deal with this anxiety that will affect your performance and your enjoyment.

Why use visualisation for competing?

- Learn how to manage your competition day nerves and reduce the pressure you may normally feel.

- Learn to focus and cut out distractions.
- To help learn your dressage test.
- To improve your movements and techniques.
- To familiarise yourself with the show scenario.
- To build your confidence through preparation.

The thought of attending a competition can be very daunting. This can also be true for your horse, a lot of horses find the experience of the unfamiliar surroundings of a show setting stressful too. Your horse will need you more than ever to give him confidence.

For example, If you are at a competition, your nerves can transfer to your horse, so can impair your performance. You may perform perfectly at home, but as soon as you get to the show ring you go to pieces, which makes your horse on edge too; neither of you can perform at your best under these conditions.

Using visualisation regularly will enable you to put yourself into a confident, positive state, which will be really helpful to fend off those competition day nerves. If you can learn to control your emotions, it will mean you and your horse will be able to perform better.

To get yourself into a competition mindset, and prepare yourself, try some visualisation techniques. Away from your horse, you can mentally prepare yourself by using images and short films inside your mind, a bit like day dreaming.

If you want to use the technique to help with competition day nerves, then you can imagine the scenario of you and your horse warming up and entering the ring, keeping in a calm, focused and confident state. Practising this at home without your horse is really effective. In your mind you will sow the seeds, so that when you are at the show, your unconscious will remember what you have visualised, and you will be able to use the calm, confident state you have practised at home.

By taking the time to prepare thoroughly, you will avoid the feelings of being overwhelmed when you are at the show. Because you have rehearsed it in your mind so many times, you will become so familiar with what will happen, it will feel as though you have already done it.

You can address any issues that might crop up, just by imaging how you should react.

Try this exercise:

1. Sit down somewhere quiet without distractions.

2. Picture yourself at the competition. Make sure you are picturing how you would like to be, without the nerves present.

3. Use all your senses, build up a complete picture, you really need to immerse yourself in the experience.

4. Picture yourself with your horse, both of you calm and confident.

5. Imagine how you will feel entering the arena, com-

pletely focused on your performance.

6. Imagine the smell of the arena, the feel of the weather, maybe the sun on your face, or the feel of the breeze, how the reins feel in your hands, imagine the feel of stroking your horses neck, what sounds can you hear. The more immersive you make the experience, the more successful it will be.

7. Visualise your success. (I don't necessarily mean winning here, success is not only measured by coming first; success may be just completing the test).

8. Take your time and really get into it, create small films of you and your horse performing at your best.

9. Practice this regularly. Close your eyes and play your film of you and your horse having fun at the show.

Combined with your physical training, you will find your progress accelerates, and your confidence around the competition will grow.

Design a plan for both yourself and your horse. Use the goal setting strategy set out in this book. Your end goal will be the competition date, and your starting point is now. Look at the date that you would like to enter your first competition, and work backwards. If you are returning to competition, you may want to enter a lower level to build your confidence back up.

From a practical point of view, both you and your horse will need to get your fitness levels up. You will need to gradually increase your horse's workload to bring him up to fitness. Just like us, this needs to be done progressively, to avoid injury. You will also need to include some technical training in your goal setting, whether this is dressage related or jumping, depending on your chosen discipline.

It can be hard to remember all of you aids/responses to a movement in real time when you are riding, especially in a competition environment. Visualising is great for memorising dressage tests and also for riding movements correctly. For example, you can visualise your entire dressage test as you would like it to go. Practice doing this in real time, so if your test is 5 minutes then visualise it as 5 minutes. (At first it will take longer than 5 minutes, as you work through the process you will be able to shorten it as described previously).

If you learn to visualise your movements correctly in your mind, step by step, then when you come to ride the movement in reality, you will have more chance of success, so when you get back in the saddle, your reactions will be exactly as you pictured them.

## Overcoming possible problems

Visualisation can help you confront a problem by imagining it, and working through it. By dealing with your problems in this way, you can ensure that you are mentally prepared beforehand, so you can preempt your responses, and find solutions.

By talking through every detail of an exercise you can plan your reactions to possible problems and how you will react, this will prevent the 'panic' which often occurs when things go wrong. This technique is a great way to cope with situations which normally unnerve you. If your horse always spooks at a certain place, you can practice how you will react in advance, and be prepared. Learning to cope with problems before they happen will mean that you do not panic when you are riding. Success in is mental planning.

This technique can be used for all common riding problems you are experiencing:

- Outline the problem; choose an issue that you would like to work on. Write down what the problem is that you would like to change.

- Present reactions; write down how you react at the moment when this problem occurs.

- Turn the present reactions into the correct reactions. Write down how you would like to react, and how you should react to the problem in the correct way. Change each of the negative reactions you are using at the moment into a positive reaction. Work through it step by step, using all of your senses. It helps to picture it in your mind as a short film. Practice replaying it until you feel confident.

Next time the problem occurs you will be ready to recall the correct reaction. Think of a short formula that will prompt you while you are riding. When you have a good experience with your horse, remember to reinforce it by running through it again in your mind to capture how you are feeling. You will soon build new positive behaviour in both yourself and your horse.

Visualisation should be practised regularly to ensure the best results.

Visualisation can also help you create new behaviours; try this exercise:

1. Identify a behaviour you would like to have. Be clear what the outcome should mean for you.

2. See yourself in the future (disassociated) with the desired behaviour, actually doing it. Disassociated means to picture yourself as though you are watching from the outside, so you are the star of your own film.

3. Be your own film director and make any changes to what you are viewing, adjusting aspects of the vision and behaviour, until the whole presentation is as perfect, smooth and

comfortable as possible (remain disassociated).

4.   Now step into this 'future you' (associated). You are now putting yourself into the film. See it through your own eyes. Really immerse yourself and experience it through as many senses as possible.

This can take some practice to be able to do; a good way to visualise it is to imagine you are sitting in a cinema and the screen is where you are creating your film.

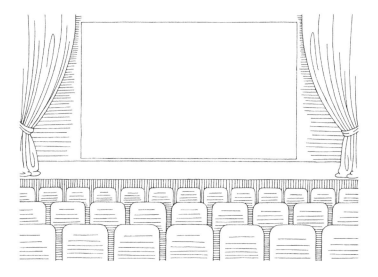

# CHAPTER 6:
# RELAXATION

## A brief but important note about relaxation

Relaxation reduces the build up of tension and stress levels, promotes rest, recovery and recuperation. Scientists have found that regular periods of deep relaxation increases the immune system, speeds up the healing process, and even reduces the risk of heart disease. To get the most benefit from the mental techniques you will learn throughout this book, it is important to learn how to relax, as it promotes a physical and mental state which increases the success of positive mental imagery and suggestion.

## Benefits of relaxation

- Reduces the build up of tension and reduces stress levels in body and mind
- Scientists have found that regular periods of deep relaxation increases the immune system, speeds up the healing process, even reduces the risk of heart disease
- Helps to cope with mood swings, anxiety and depression and is used by mainstream psychologists
- Breathing slows
- Muscles relax
- Blood pressure regulates to natural 'resting' levels
- Heart rate becomes slow and regular
- Blood circulation changes to 'healing mode'
- Visualisation skills are enhanced
- Unconscious mind becomes more dominant and open

to suggestion and positive images
- Conscious mind relaxes to prevent over analysing (still alert enough to prevent improper suggestion)
- Endorphin levels increase, reducing pain and tension, and create a sense of healing and well being

## Muscle relaxation

To achieve muscle relaxation you need to actively contract and relax each of your muscles, tightening the muscle for 4-6 seconds and then relaxing it, which leaves the muscle in a more relaxed state than it started. Do this to each body part in turn. Feet, legs, thighs, buttocks, stomach, back, neck, shoulders, arms, hands, jaw, face and eyes. A relaxed muscle state will make you feel warm and heavy.

Relaxation techniques also involve breathing techniques, concentrating on control and regulation.

## Breathing technique

Learning diaphragmatic or 'belly' breathing is a great way of managing the symptoms of anxiety and panic. It is the act of breathing deeply into your lungs by flexing your diaphragm rather than breathing shallowly by flexing your rib cage. It is generally considered a healthier and fuller way to ingest oxygen and is often used as a therapy for anxiety disorders. We automatically breathe this way when we are born, if you watch a baby breathing you will notice their stomach rising and falling.

Relearning to use your diaphragm in breathing is important in managing the symptoms of anxiety and panic.

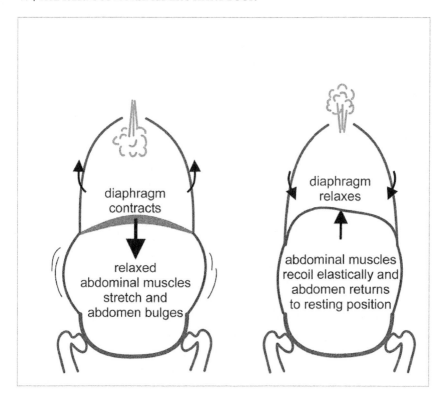

To achieve this method of breathing you need to practice. When you do, you will find that it completely relaxes your body and mind. Done properly, your muscles won't be able to tense up, and you can use it on demand when you need it. It is really helpful to do before you ride, as often, if you are feeling a little nervous or tense, you forget to breath deeply, resulting in your muscles tensing up when you are on board your horse, which will transfer to your horse. So by breathing steadily and deeply, together with the effect of your relaxed muscles, your horse will relax much easier too.

To perform this exercise:

1. Sit or lie comfortably.

2. Put one hand on your chest and one on your stomach.

3. Slowly inhale through your nose.

4. As you inhale, feel your stomach expand with your hand.

5.  Slowly exhale through your lips to regulate the release of air.

6. Rest and repeat.

Once you are proficient you can easily perform diaphragmatic breathing while standing, or sitting on your horse.

## Self hypnosis routine for relaxation

Simply relaxing into a light state of trance is extremely good for you. Known as 'Alpha State', the relaxation process is similar to the state you slip into just before you go to sleep, or during wakening; it is similar to day dreaming. During the Alpha state your mind is clear and open to thoughts and realisations, and is at an optimum state.

You can be extremely relaxed and still be 'in control'. If you needed to be alert quickly for whatever reason, you could just snap out of it and be awake and in your normal state. You cannot get stuck in a state of relaxation or hypnosis. If you go deeper, you simply fall asleep.

**Safety warning:** Do not use the self-hypnosis routine outlined below in a moving vehicle, while operating machinery, while bathing in a bath or pool, or in any place or occasion where being non-alert or sleepy might present a hazard.

Before you start, read the safety warning above, and double check that it is safe to proceed. Then ensure you are in a safe, comfortable and relaxing position, where you will not be disturbed. Loosen any tight belt, tie, shoe laces or clothing if possible.

1. Begin by either sitting or lying comfortably, if possible with

    a gently straight back.
2. Take a deep breath in, filling your lungs.
3. Release it out.
4. Repeat the deep breath for 5-10 repetitions.
5. Close your eyes and continue to breathe deeply.
6. Let your awareness drift down into your feet. Feel their natural weight.
7. Imagine your feet growing heavier in a nice, comfortable way.
8. Let the weight spread up into your calves and shins, relaxing all the little muscles there.
9. Let the weight spread up over and through your knees, relaxing them.
10. Let the weight spread up into your thighs, relaxing them.
11. Let the weight spread up into all the muscles around your tummy, abdomen, lower back and sides.
12. Let the weight spread up gently into your chest. Notice your chest and shoulders feeling heavy with out-breaths, and floating up with in-breaths.
13. Let the weight spread down your arms, leaving arms, hands and fingers feeling heavy.
14. Let the weight spread up into your neck, relaxing neck and shoulders.
15. Let the weight spread up into your face, relaxing all the little muscles around eyes, mouth and cheeks.
16. Let the weight spread up around your temples, leaving temples and forehead smooth and relaxed.
17. Let the weight spread up into your scalp, as if a heavy, warm, comfortable massage was happening there.
18. Let the weight double slowly all the way down your body back down to your toes.
19. Let yourself imagine a relaxing pleasant scene in a safe and relaxing place. This might be the country, seaside, anywhere safe and nice. Maybe from one of your favourite days out or holiday.
20. Imagine all the sights, sounds, smells, scents.

21. Imagine a path going off into the distance. Follow the path in a relaxed and calm way.
22. Just allow yourself to wonder what goals, successes and objectives you may begin to achieve by following that path. Now is a good time to include your positive affirmations.
23. Follow the path for as long as you wish, and then be aware that even after you awaken, you will still unconsciously be on the path.
24. When you are ready, slowly count firmly up from one to ten.
25. Stretch, slowly open your eyes, blink and have a few quiet moments before returning to full activity.
26. Do not drive, operate machinery etc. until you have had a few minutes getting fully awake, as you would from a quick cat nap.

The self hypnosis exercise is very effective to combine with your visualisation exercises. Simply insert your visualisation into steps 22 and 23.

Mindfulness and meditation are widely becoming commonplace, and if you can put aside 10 minutes a day to work through your own guided meditation, it can be hugely beneficial. You can write your own scripts, and record them to play back. Scripts are particularly effective when you are in 'Alpha State', such as during relaxation. Only include good positive language, such as 'I am', and avoid words such as 'hope' and 'try'.

# CHAPTER 7: NEGATIVE TO POSITIVE

A negative thought only takes hold of you if you let it; by reacting to it and giving it emotion. By identifying your negative thoughts and changing them into positives, you can start to overcome the 'what ifs'. Get into the habit of being aware of how you are talking to yourself internally, and make sure you are kind to yourself.

**Negative to positive**

It is very easy to get into a circle of negativity with your horse. You feel anxious and give off nervous signals, your horse picks up on these and tenses up, which makes you even more anxious, which in turn transfers again to your horse, and so it goes on... For example; your horse sees something he cannot identify up ahead, and goes 'up on his toes'; in response, you tighten up the reins and tense in the saddle, staring in the same direction, your horse reads this as you also being greatly concerned about the 'monster' hiding ahead. This confirms his fear, puts him more on his toes and activates his flight response, which in turn makes you even more anxious, creating a negative cycle. Your horse, being a prey animal, needs you, his rider, 'the herd leader' to tell him there is no monster to worry about, which will settle him down, build trust and give him the confidence to keep riding past. Obviously, this is easier said than done if you are suffering from a lack of confidence, but highlights the importance of confidence where there are two living creatures involved, the horse needs to feed from the rider's confidence as you are representing the 'herd leader'.

The only way to stop this perpetual cycle is from you changing the way you react. When you feel the results from your horse's reaction in response, it will spur you on to continue. You need to practice putting yourself in a 'confident state' before you get on your horse, as it can be difficult to concentrate once you are caught in your negative cycle, your mind tends to be blocked by this stage. You can't rely on your horse to make the first move to be confident because they are a prey animal and look to you as their herd leader, they need to feed from your confidence.

When you keep thinking negative thoughts, you create a self fulfilling prophecy, causing a downward spiral. So the more you think of not being able to control your horse, or thinking you are going to fall off, or that your riding is rubbish, the more likely these things are to become true. This is because automatically accepting these negative beliefs, even though they are distorted and irrational, influences the way you view yourself. Once a negative belief is activated, your thoughts shift away from the positive, and you will then distort further incoming information to fit into your negative state of mind. Riders need to develop an ability to ride in the present. This means accepting any mistakes or negative experiences and immediately dismissing them. Focusing on what went wrong increases the chances of it happening again, so always pick out what was good about an exercise or training session, even one that went wrong, focus on the positives and say what you will improve next time.

You can learn to control your emotional response. To do this you need to change your perception of these situations and the way you think about them, which will change the way you feel and behave. The way you interpret situations, and think and feel about them affects your behaviour. Anxiety promotes negative thinking. Identifying this and changing your thinking patterns can relieve the anxiety you are feeling.

To really make effective changes, you need to make a concerted effort. Modern research has revealed that the brain never stops changing in response to learning, and can re-wire itself.

Challenge your negative beliefs about yourself, examine the evidence for and against, this will enable you to find an alternative scenario to the negative thought.

Focusing on solutions, not problems, will shift your focus. By focusing your attention on your problem, you will just make that problem bigger. Negativity breeds negativity. Start to focus on possible solutions and you will soon attract the answers. Positivity breeds positivity.

Use this quick exercise to get the ball rolling to turn your negative thoughts into positives:

**Releasing negative thoughts**

1.  Describe in words any negative or unpleasant feelings you are having.

2.  Write down the negative thoughts you are experiencing.

3.  Define the event or situations that trigger these emotions.

4.  Describe alternative positive ways to respond to the trigger.

## Neural pathways

Up until the 1960s, researchers believed that changes in the brain could only take place during infancy and childhood. At this time it was believed that by early adulthood, the brain's physical structure was mostly permanent. Neuroscientists now know that the brain never stops changing, and recent research shows that the brain continues to create new neural pathways and alter existing ones in order to adapt to new experiences, learn new information and create new memories.

You do not need to have a great understanding of neural pathways to be able to reap the benefits of how they work. Just to know that by altering your thought patterns, your nerve cells will relay different information to your brain and feed you different emotions and behaviours in return.

Neurons (nerve cells) relay information to the brain from every part of the body. The brain then processes the information, and then sends signals through motor nerve cells back to the body to create a response/action. This is done through neural pathways, and it happens during learning, and basically everything that we do. (For things we do automatically, the neural pathways are well established and traveled). When learning something new, a new neural pathway is created.

We create neural pathways every time we learn something new. An example that most people can relate to is learning to drive. At first, you have to concentrate on every small thing. Over time and repetition, it starts to become automatic. This is because through repetition, you have formed a strong neural pathway, and so you can perform automatically.

Our brains' form neural pathways in a way that is similar to the formation of a well traveled hiking path. An easier way to understand this is to imagine yourself walking along a path through the woods. The pathway is clear and well trodden. Now imagine that this path represents your current actions/learning/experiences, this is the path that you always follow.

If you want to change your current reactions to a situation then you need to make new pathways in your mind, which will replace the old pathways, and therefore create a more positive reaction and response, switching off the old response.

To do this, imagine that you decide to take a different route (by this I mean you need to imagine a new way you would like to think about the situation, the feelings you would like to have, and new ways you would like to react), and make a new path through the woodland, treading down the undergrowth. At first, this new route is difficult, but if you now decided to always take this new route instead of the other path, this new route would soon become a well trodden path, leaving the other path to become overgrown and unusable. This new path represents your new neural pathway that you have made by changing your actions/thoughts/learning.

Neurons (nerve cells) that are used frequently develop stronger connections and those that are rarely or never used eventually fade.

## Basic first steps of rewiring your brain to be more positive

If you find yourself generally focusing on what may go wrong all the time and thinking negatively, there is a simple exercise you can begin to use straight away on your own:

1. Address each negative thought one at a time.

2. For each negative thought, replace it with three positive thoughts.

3. This will give your brain a kick-start into rewiring itself.

4. Once you change these thoughts, your feelings and behaviours will follow suit.

## How long does it take for you to notice an effect?

Like changing a habit, it takes a while to establish a regular pattern of positiveness. On average it usually takes around 30 days to cement in place, if done consistently. Repetition is the key to success here. Using repetition will change the neural pathways in your brain and the new thinking will become normal. Stick with it, its bound to be hard to start with, like learning any new skill. The more you do it, the easier it becomes. Like when you learn to drive, and at first you have to be really conscious of changing gear and how to do it, but after a while it becomes second nature; or in equestrian terms, when you learn to ride it is difficult to coordinate all of your aids, after a period of time, you can just use them without thinking.

## Habits

Habits are formed gradually over time. This is the same for good habits as unwanted habits. A habit is a behaviour that is automatic because it has been performed many times. Your unconscious likes habits because it controls your automatic responses. You can speak to your unconscious to change any unwanted habits and their automatic responses.

To make a habit you need to create an automatic behaviour pattern. Obviously at first this is a sustained, conscious effort, and then over time the habit becomes ingrained in your everyday life, and is easier to execute and continue. This repetition creates a mental association between the trigger and the behaviour, which means that each time the trigger is encountered, the behaviour is performed automatically.

To replace an unwanted behaviour, first identify your trigger. Your habit will happen after a cue. What you need to do is replace this behaviour with a more favourable behaviour to the trigger.

The key to successfully making a new habit stick is in understanding how habits are formed. The following principles apply to whatever habit you want to establish.

- Always use positives for your habit. Do not say what you don't want to be doing, always use positive language. Your brain will not learn anything by 'not doing' something, it needs something new 'to do'.

- Visualise yourself succeeding. Imagine yourself reacting with your new responses and how it will feel.

- Having a cue is important. Develop a new habit in response to a cue. For example, you may decide that your morning coffee is your cue, and set up your new habit to be associated with that time.

- Make your new habit achievable. So at first, break it down, start small and set the bar low. Especially if you have been suffering from low self esteem, and do not feel confident in your ability to execute new behaviours, which is very common.

- A less challenging habit will be easier to succeed with at first, and then when you feel comfortable at this level, you can gradually grow to what you want to achieve. This method will prevent stress overload. An example that is easy for a lot of people to relate to is getting fit. You may want to be able to run a marathon, and you may think you should do a certain amount of running to get where you want to be, but it is difficult to sustain this, if it is where you start. Instead, a much better way to be successful is to just start off small, say a 20 minute walk each day, the next week up it to 1 hour. Then twice a week do 30 minutes of walk with short jogs along the way. You can build up gradually like this, and are more likely to succeed, for many reasons, including the reward you will feel from achieving the smaller goal each day, plus you will not be too physically exhausted, or overwhelmed at first to continue again.

. Have a plan in place for when things go wrong. For example, if you want to eat more healthily. You are bound to slip up at some point and break your habit. In this instance you should factor in a couple of times a week, where you allow yourself to have an unhealthy meal, or snack. Have this in your plan. This will stop you going off track on your good days, as you know you have a couple of slots that you are allowed to have that more unhealthy option. Also you will not have to feel as though you have failed, because you are allowed to do it in your plan. This will establish your willpower. It would be unrealistic to expect yourself to eat healthy 100% of the time, and would lead to you not sticking to the habit.

. Think of the ways you might slip, and put in place a plan so you can keep on track. If it is work related, and you are prone to procrastinating, allow yourself a couple of short times in the day when you allocate time slots to having a break from work to browse the internet, or play a game. Just keep to the rules you have set. For the same reasons as above, this will prevent you from feelings of failure and establish your willpower, as you wait until the time you have allotted.

When you switch to a new pattern of behaviour, each time you succeed just a little bit, you will be rewarded. Your brain will log your new experience, giving you a good feeling, which will spur you on to continue again. This is why little steps work so well to get you started.

Once your habits are ingrained, you will not be conscious of the great effort at exerting your willpower, this is because your brain will have created new neural pathways from your new habit. You will stop having to make yourself think about everything and your habitual behaviour will become automatic (known as un-conscious competence).

## How to break an unhealthy habit

The key is to replace the unwanted habit with a new healthier habit.

1. Identify your behaviour and your trigger, this in itself will help you find ways to change it and react in a more positive way. Stop saying what you are not going to do, instead use positive language and say what you are going to do. The language you use is incredibly powerful. Your brain will not learn anything by 'not doing' something, it needs something new 'to do'. You can only succeed in breaking a bad habit when you focus on a new good habit to replace the behaviour.

2. It is important to have a plan of what you will do next time you are faced with your trigger. Define a different response to the trigger.

3. Investigate what your triggers are and realistically which ones you can avoid. Examine the feelings you get from the trigger and come up with counter arguments for them. Have a debate with yourself and find alternative responses.

4. Visualise yourself succeeding. Imagine yourself reacting with your new responses and how it will feel.

5.    You need to return to a time when you didn't have the unhealthy reactions. There will have been a time in your life when you didn't feel this way. You are already capable of the positive behaviour, and it's important to get this into perspective.

## Method

1.    Write down your new response each day for 30 days. This reinforces it in your mind. Say it out loud too. Your unconscious likes repetition. Use self hypnosis to describe the feelings of the new habit, to ingrain them in your unconscious, therefore giving it a better chance to search for the positive automatic responses to the new habit.

2.    Focus on the positive instead of the negative, use visualisation techniques to help you. Repetition of the positive will empower your thoughts, feelings and emotions to move away from the negative emotions and into the new positive state. You are forcing your brain to redirect. Negative – STOP – Positive.

3.    Overcome negative self-talk. Use positive phrases when talking to yourself, if you feel yourself being critical and defeatist, then immediately follow this up with saying something positive to yourself.

4.    Plan for things that can go wrong, it's ok to have stumbling blocks, this is reality, it just means you need to find another way that works better for you. Do not beat yourself up about it, just get back on track and try again. This is what successful people do.

5.    Be aware of your thoughts and feelings, tune in to your thoughts, if they are negative then change them and redirect them to more positives.

Be patient, to form a new habit can take a minimum of 28 days, but in reality it can take longer than this to become automatic. Start now and stick with it, it may seem like a long time, but time goes pretty quickly. As you go along it will get easier, even though it may be difficult when you first begin.

## Reframing

Reframing is a straightforward and easy to use mental training technique which is particularly useful to horse riders, but can also be used to help in all areas of your life with great results. When you reframe something, you find an alternative thinking pattern.

Hopefully by now you can see the underlying theme of mental training. To turn your negative mindset into a more positive mindset, to retrain your thinking patterns, and in turn your behaviour responses.

Firstly, lets look at what we mean by framing. A frame is a way of perceiving something to give it a meaning, the perceptions we have surrounding events or behaviours. Our perceptions may not be based on fact, but on feelings. The meaning of an event depends on how we frame it. Not only on past events, but we also have preconceptions on future ones. We judge how that experience might be, even before it has happened. We might avoid experiences because of how we frame them, when they may have, in fact, been positive for us. Framing things in a certain way can lead to negative patterns, so that you will repeat the behaviour and develop toxic thinking patterns.

Reframing is changing the context of the current frame to give something another meaning. When you reframe, you change the meaning, so your responses and behaviour will change too. It gives you more choices.

Try this exercise:

1. Think of an experience you have had where you would like to

change your behaviour in that situation.

2. Now identify alternative behaviours to that situation that you would like to use when you have the experience again in the future. Try to think of 3 responses.

3. Now think again of the experience using your new behaviours in place of your old behaviour.

4. You should now be able to see the experience from a different perspective, keep thinking of this new version.

5. By doing this, you have now reframed the experience, and the emotions attached to it.

# CHAPTER 8: OVER-HORSED?

Being over-horsed is where a rider's current skill level is not matched to the requirements of their horse. The amateur horse rider will no doubt have been in this situation at some point.

This is a very sensitive area to address. It can be difficult for a rider to admit to themselves that they are not coping with their horse. This is such a common occurrence, that it is necessary to address it in a book about confidence issues. And indeed, lack of confidence can often be credited directly to a rider being in this situation.

A rider should be matched to a horse within their ability level. A novice rider is much more suited to a quite, older cob, than a younger thoroughbred. For a lot of riders, they decide to embark on buying their first horse after they have had some lessons at a riding school, and, after finding themselves absolutely falling in love with being around the horses, decide to look for their own. Often riders don't tend to realise what generous animals the riding school horses are. Although they may have some tricks up their sleeves, they are ultimately forgiving when it comes to the novice rider, and know their job extremely well.

I know this may sound harsh, but it is a stark warning to potential horse owners. A combination of a novice rider, and a difficult, or young horse, is not healthy for either party, and can be dangerous. It will certainly quickly deplete any confidence you had built up. Your first horse needs to be a steady, well mannered schoolmaster. You should really avoid young, inexperienced horses, ex-racehorses, ex-eventers or horses described as 'not a novice ride'.

It's a bit like when you buy your first car after learning to drive. What you should really get is a car that is not too powerful and is easy to handle, like a Ford Fiesta, and not a Subaru or a Dodge Viper!

All horses are different and individual. Being over-horsed does not mean you have a 'naughty' or 'dangerous' horse, it simply means that at this current time, you may not have the level of experience needed.

If you find yourself in this situation, and feel out of your depth, then you know how much anxiety it can cause. To move forward from this, you will need to seek professional advice.

Firstly, you need to be honest. There is nothing to be ashamed or embarrassed about. Instructors see this situation all the time. Never be afraid to ask for help.

A professional can assess your situation and make sure you are not putting yourself in any danger. Sometimes all that is needed is some coaching to increase your skill set and experience, if you are happy and willing to put the time and effort into this adventure. Some riders are suited to the challenge, and others prefer to seek another solution. It may be that you can have your horse professionally schooled, whilst having lessons yourself on a more suitable mount. But bear in mind, that just having your horse re-schooled, may not in itself improve your partnership. You will also need to embrace training for yourself too, and invest the time to become an even better rider. Once you have weighed up all the options, what you decide to do, is ultimately, a very personal choice.

In some cases, rider's have decided to sell their horse to someone who has more experience, and can bring out the best in that horse. This does not mean you do not 'love' your horse, or have failed in some way; you are doing what is in the best interests for both of you. This can be for many reasons, and not only skill related.

Often rider's have found that when they move onto another horse, they are much better suited and they start to enjoy riding again, as their confidence increases.

## How to avoid purchasing a horse above your ability

If you have decided to take the plunge into the exciting world of owning a horse, then make sure you do some thorough research of what you are getting into. There is so much behind the scenes that you may be unaware of, both financially and physically. I am not trying to put anyone off of owning a horse, it is just best to go into it with your eyes wide open.

A lot of riding schools and equestrian colleges run horse knowledge and care courses, which are great for prospective horse owners. They will give you a good understanding of what is involved to look after your own horse. Sharing or part loaning a horse is also a good option to see if you are ready for horse owner-ship.

Unfortunately, for the novice, the horse buying experience can be where it all goes wrong. Rider's often buy beyond their capabilities. This is not always the fault of the buyer. Purchasing a horse can be a minefield. Not every seller is completely honest; I have know many cases where the horses are actually sedated when the buyer goes to view and try them, to hide poor training or behavioural issues; or lameness is disguised using painkillers.

You want to make sure that the kind hearted, sound, healthy horse that you viewed, is the same horse when you come home with it.

Here are a few pointers to remember when you go out and view a potential horse:

- Its a huge purchase, so take your time, don't feel like you are a nuisance, you really need to get a good, thorough picture of the horse's personality, behaviour, health and soundness, both on the ground, and ridden.

- Take an experienced horse person with you.

- Ask lots of questions; about the horse's history, where they bought it from, and how long they have owned the horse, any illnesses & injuries, temperament, how are they with hacking, loading, catching, clipping, how they are with the farrier and vet, how are they with shows, and ask the reason why they are selling the horse.

- Handle the horse from the ground yourself.

- See the horse being tacked up, ask the owner not to get the horse ready before you arrive, you really want to see what it is like with grooming, picking its feet up, and coming out of the stable.

- Ask the seller to ride the horse first. Never get on the horse first. Ask them to show you all it's paces, and pop over a small jump if appropriate.

- Ask to see the horse's passport and vaccination record.

It is a legal requirement that a horse is sold with a passport. From October 2020 it is mandatory for all owners to microchip their horses, so check there is a record of this.

- Before you commit, have a pre-purchase veterinary examination done.

- Do not buy on impulse.

- The right horse for you is out there, be patient.

Genuine sellers will be happy to provide you with as much detail about the horse as you ask. They should care as much as you do about the horse's future welfare.

# CHAPTER 9: CONFIDENCE AND RIDING

Recap and put together everything you have learned so far. Practice all your mental training and build some plans of how you can proceed forwards.

When you ride you have an open channel of communication with your horse, he is constantly asking you questions, and you are answering him through your body language, he will pick up on everything you are feeling.

Your state of mind has a direct effect on how your horse reacts to you. Without a positive riding mind, your position and aids become ineffective. Thinking positively causes you to relax, be much clearer and more definite with your aids, and you will find your horse will settle much easier when you are calm. Tell yourself "I can do this, I am in control", don't let any doubts creep into your mind. You need to be in a 'confident state' when you are with your horse.

Through positive thinking your body language will change. Your horse will normally display a mirror image of how you are feeling, he is extremely sensitive to the slightest change in your muscle tension, breathing and nervous energy. If you panic, your horse will panic. Remember, negativity is wasted energy; when you are tense you tend to breath very shallow (or hold your breath altogether), which is exhausting in itself.

Breathing deeply and slowly, and feeling your stomach rise and fall will lower your heart rate and calm you down. This way your horse feels you are relaxed, so will relax too in response. If you practice your deep breathing everyday, you will find that you can easily replicate this when you are on your horse, to reset yourself, and instantly relax your muscles.

Having specific plans for each session you spend at the stables with your horse will really help you to progress and give you structure, keeping your mind occupied and move you away from your 'over thinking' brain and the 'what ifs'.

When you are riding, you need to shut out all distractions, focus all your energy on the task now, be in the now, don't get side tracked. Concentrate on what lies immediately ahead, shut out the past and future. Put any problems away in a box in your mind, to deal with later, after you have ridden.

You need to develop this ability to ride in the present, which means accepting any mistakes and immediately dismissing them. Focusing on what went wrong increases the chance of it happening again. Remember to always pick out what was good about an exercise, focus on the positives.

**Some tips for increasing your ridden confidence:**

- Do lots of groundwork with your horse to develop your relationship and trust.

- Develop a correct, balanced and secure position. Feeling that you can maintain your balance through different movements and transitions will increase your confidence. Go back to basics, it really is fundamental to everything else you do and should not be overlooked. Remember every time you ride your horse you are training him, so by going back to basics, you may resolve some of the problems that you may be having now.

- Mastering the basics is fundamental to increasing confidence, developing a secure, balanced position will make you feel safe. Riding skills should not be overlooked when increasing your confidence.

- Learn how to easily stop on command with your seat and core, instead of your hands. It seems obvious, but learning to stop is very important to feeling confident. A lot of riders, especially when feeling anxious, tend to be ineffective at stopping, this is because in your anxious state you will lose the deepness of your seat in the saddle through perching, and may also be pulling on your reins in an effort to slow down. These methods simply won't work, your horse will just fight against them, ignore you and even speed up as your tenseness is transferred to him. Again, this is a viscous circle that can easily be rectified with forward planning and mental preparation, as we have learned throughout this book.

- Practice riding controlled downward transitions. You will then be retraining your horse to stay balanced through the transitions, which will help you to stay in balance and secure.

- When you establish a secure, balanced position, and you know you can stop on demand, you will lose your fear of riding at faster paces, and trying new things.

- Learn to develop feel; increasing body awareness is very important to develop, as it is through your body that you communicate to your horse. Its amazing how many riders are not aware of what their body is doing or feeling whilst riding. Focusing on body awareness and feel will improve your riding skills and relationship with your horse as you strive to become 'one'. Tune into each part of your body to improve awareness of how the horse feels moving underneath you. Feel your horse's strides. Get your instructor to help with your position, so you are training your body to feel in the correct place.

- Learn to use your breathing techniques while on your horse, to calm you down. Remember your relaxation and breathing techniques. You can use these both before riding and during riding to reset yourself. It is impossible to tense up whilst performing the deep breathing. Get in the habit of taking a few deep breaths when you have first mounted, and are walking your horse around. He will immediately feel at ease too; your horse is completely in tune with your muscle tension and breathing.

- Learn to relax your muscles to 'fake' relaxation, thereby, sending positive vibes to your horse.

- Learn to control your emotions around your horse. Horses are so sensitive to us, they even match heartbeats.

- Go at your own pace, set yourself small goals.

- Ride in the present, don't think about the past or the future. Worrying about something that happened in the past, or fears of what might happen in the future distract riders from focusing on what is happening now. Develop the ability to accept and dismiss immediately any mistakes, you cannot change the past, so put it out of your mind.

- Focus on what you do want to happen, not what you don't, as this negative thought pattern can make the negatives more likely. When thoughts are negative, stop and refocus on your goal and how to get there. Take action on negative thoughts.

- Don't push yourself into a high anxiety position, take

small steps and gain confidence first. It is ok to stretch yourself, but try not to enter the 'panic zone'.

- Use visualisation before you ride. Visualisation allows you to focus, shut out distractions and get things 'right', as you have already acted out what you will do in your mental rehearsal.

- Plan for how to cope with possible problems.

- Use your 'thought stopping' technique if you feel any negatives creeping into your mind as you are riding.

- List positives about yourself as a rider. If you think of any negatives, turn each negative belief into a positive one and write them down.

## Play your visualisation as a video in your mind

If you have been working through the book, you will now have many resources to draw upon. Your scripts/videos/imagery can now be used in practice when you are riding. Plan ahead and run through your visualisation of how you want your session to play out. Just to recap: scientific studies have found that the muscles and the unconscious mind cannot distinguish between visualised activity and actual activity. This means that, through visualisation practice, you can train yourself to react in the correct way automatically, and then you will be able to override your 'panic reaction'. This method is very effective.

By talking through every detail of an exercise you can plan your reactions to possible problems and how you will react, this will prevent the 'panic' which often occurs when things go wrong. This technique is a great way to cope with situations which normally unnerve you.

You may be thinking, how is this possible, I can't just pretend I am confident, my horse will know. But your horse does not know what you are actually thinking, he reacts to your muscle tension, heart rate and physical actions. Just as negative behaviour sets you on a downward spiral; positive behaviour will set you on an upward spiral. You will experience emotional rewards when you do this, as your horse reacts in a calmer, more positive way. You will find that as you take small steps towards becoming more confident, with each small triumph, you will experience this emotional reward, which will fuel you to carry on.

You will soon be on the road to full confidence. Once you start the process and receive the emotional rewards, it will spur you on to continue. You will then begin to feel the power of your confidence building take effect.

## Remember 'feelings are not facts'

The way you feel is not who you are. You must not let the way you feel lead you to believe that that is who you are. How you are feeling is not how you will always be, feelings change all the time.

## Building experience

One thing it is important to remember is that experiences build confidence. The more you do towards your goal, even tiny steps, will build your confidence. Every positive experience you have will be stored away and built up into a bank of memories to draw upon as you move forward.

When you start to move forward with your horse, and are thinking about riding, preparation is key to helping your confidence. Preparation cannot be overstated when it comes to confidence building, especially if you are working alone. The more you prepare for each time you are at the stables, the more competent and less nervous you will feel.

Remember, horses live in the moment, and learn through association. The horse is capable of any movement and is completely in balance without a rider, you only have to watch them playing in the field to witness fantastic dressage moves. When you put a rider on his back, he has to rebalance himself, which he can only achieve if the rider is responsible for their own body, and they are in balance themselves. The rider must therefore carry themselves and support their own weight so as not to interfere with the horse.

When horse and rider find harmony, everything else seems easy and effortless.

**What is your most important aid on a horse?**

You may be thinking the answer is legs, seat, hands? But in fact it is your brain, your mind is the most important aid that you have.

Confident riders still get negative thoughts, but they know how to shut off these negative internal dialogues and replace them with positives. They have trained themselves to think of ways to encourage success, and now you also have these skills to be able to do this for yourself. Use your self talk constructively and positively.

When you are riding your horse, you should go back to basics, and really develop a secure, balanced position to give yourself extra confidence. The fundamentals are really key to building a partnership of trust and security with your horse.

Riding skills must not be overlooked when dealing with your fear; improving your skills, both on the ground and in the saddle will increase your confidence, as will observing safe practices. Learning more about horse behaviour and psychology will also help you to understand how your horse is behaving and responding. A lot of riders put a human perspective on their horses behaviour, but horses are not capable of thinking as we do, and cannot be compared.

When you are with your horse you must act as if you have all the time in the world. Horses have no concept of 'stress at the office', or quickly riding before dinner etc. When you rush and are stressed, it will have a negative effect on your horse. If you feel stressed, you are better to not ride your horse, and to wait until you are in a better frame of mind.

## While you are riding:

A great way to distract your mind off of any nerves, is to ride a lot of movements in your arena, keep your mind busy, and more importantly, your horse's mind busy. If you are both focused and busy, then the tension will not grow into a problem from either one of you. This is a tried and tested method, and really does make a difference.

Before your session with your horse, write your plan down, include all transitions and movements, almost as though you are designing your own dressage test.

There is nothing worse than getting your horse in the menage, and just wandering around without purpose. This is not good for either one of you, and your horse will not be paying attention to you, but he will be looking about at everything else. This will lead to you not feeling confident. Your mind will also wander and worry. If you have a plan in place, then this will not happen, you will both be in tune with one another, and will not be distracted. Try this next time you are in the menage.

Be aware of your surrounding area. Look into the distance as well as your immediate area. Taking in the vista with your eyes will help your brain deal with your nerves. Focus on the trees, really look into the distance and notice what is around you. I am not saying don't be aware of what is right in front of you, but it is important not to just focus on this, or on your horse. A lot of riders tend to look down a lot of the time, this really affects your overall balance. Keeping your eyes up, keeps your head up, and this balances you.

You need to ride in the present, this means accepting any mistakes and immediately dismissing them. It something does not go to plan, don't worry, just move on, put it out of your mind. This is where having a plan is so helpful. You can just move onto what you had planned next. At the end of your session, always pick out what was good, focus on the positives and say what you will improve next time.

Notice how you feel when you are on your horse, balanced and sitting in alignment, in halt, walk, trot, canter, through the transitions and movements. When a transition goes well remember exactly how it felt, and log the experience. Go through the feelings you got so you don't forget how it feels. Practice this each time something goes well when you are riding, and in time you will be able to recall these feelings easily, and so be able to recreate them. This is very effective.

# CHAPTER 10: PRACTICAL RIDING TIPS FOR BUILDING CONFIDENCE

Gaining an understanding of the fundamentals cannot be over emphasised when it comes to riding. The underlying principles are the same regardless of whichever discipline you choose to pursue. This is not something you should cut corners on, and is paramount to your confidence levels. Ask any successful rider, or reputable coach, and they will tell you how important good foundations are to establish.

## Body sculpting and muscle memory

Rider's are not always aware of their body position on their horse. How they are positioned can feel correct to the rider, however, often, in reality, they are sitting in an unbalanced, insecure way. For example, you may feel you are sitting in an upright position, when in fact you are leaning forward. This is very common, and it is because you feel comfortable in your current position as your muscle memory has built up, and has made the position automatic for you.

Work on your riding position should always start with your seat. Make sure you are sitting equally on each seat bone, as this will place you centrally in the saddle. Move your seat around a bit if you have trouble feeling them. When you are in closest contact with the saddle you will feel the two bony protrusions underneath you.

Increasing your body awareness is so important to develop, as it is through your body that you communicate to your horse. It's amazing how many riders are not aware of what their body is doing or feeling whilst riding. Focusing on body awareness and feel will improve your riding skills and relationship with your horse, as you strive to become 'one'. Tune in to each part of your body to improve your awareness of how the horse feels moving underneath you. Feel your horse's strides. If you have an instructor, ask them to help with your position so you are training your body to feel in the correct place. I use a method called 'body sculpting' for this, which really makes the rider aware of where their body should be, in this way your muscles will build a muscle memory, and will, with time, sit in this new position automatically. Scan your body as it is, noticing each part individually, notice how it feels. Now imagine, as fully as you can, how you want your position to be; in your mind create this ideal position. Hold the image, now move into this new body, adjust any areas of your body to feel as you imagined the perfect position to be, maybe get your instructor to help with this. Notice how each part of your body now feels in this new position, notice every individual part of your body, first at the halt, then try doing the same thing at walk, trot and eventually canter, obviously running through the imagery, including the movement of yourself with the horse. Bu using this method you can tune into individual parts of your body and be able to develop 'feel'. As my riders agree, it feels strange at first, but after a short period of time, you will begin to 'sculpt' yourself when you get on your horse. Eventually you will be able to simultaneously 'feel' all of your body moving its individual parts, instead of feeling one stiff position.

**Would you land on your feet if your horse disappeared**

## from underneath you?

If you are correctly positioned on your horse, then you are responsible for your own body weight, and would land on your feet if your horse were to disappear; you are aligned with your shoulder, hip and heel, and not interfering with your horse at all. This is optimal, and what you should aim for. If you feel you would fall forward, then you are sitting too perched, tipping your horse onto his forehand, or, if on the other hand you would fall backwards, then you are behind the movement. The reason this is important is because it means you are in balance, which makes you more secure and therefore increases your confidence. If you are tipped too far forward or backwards then you are not in control of your own body, and will feel unstable whilst riding, and your horse is having to carry your weight, and this will unbalance him too.

Find your balance so that you are not moving more than your horse. You are aiming to work with your horse's movement, and not against it. Feel each stride and go with it. Picture yourself as one, and not two separate beings. This way you will find harmony.

When you move together you will feel very secure, it is when you are in front or behind the movement of your horse, that you will get thrown about and lose your balance. Again, this is why going back to basics and making sure you have the fundamentals correct is so important.

## The roles of your seat

A passive seat is a following seat, you're just following your horse's movement, to maintain the stride.

A driving seat indicates a change of gait, but you should only push once.

A still (restraining) seat controls the rhythm, length of stride and all downwards transitions. To still your seat, tighten your tummy muscles to stop your hips, telling your horse to slow or stop.

## Learn to stop your horse with your seat

Using your still seat, make yourself heavy by relaxing your back and opening your hips to spread your seat, so you feel as much contact with the saddle as possible. Use a restricting rein, not a pulling rein, so just keep your hands still. If your horse is particularly strong, then just give and take with a slight tightening of your fingers around the rein. This will teach your horse to stop. Your horse's mouth is very sensitive, you do not need to pull. In fact, if you pull, you will find your horse just takes the bit and pulls against you. Your horse is much stronger than you in this situation; that is why pulling on the reins is not effective.

## How can your seat bones improve your riding?

In Europe, riders often stay on the lunge for the first year to 18 months of training, to develop a truly independent seat. Traditionally in the UK, we only stay on the lunge for a short period of time, and if we learn to ride in a group, maybe not at all.

Your seat is the most important element of your riding position. Everything else should work outwards from this central point.

Working on your riding position should always start with your seat. To know if you are sitting in the correct place, you should be able to feel both seat bones equally on the saddle. You should sit in 'neutral position', this means sitting centrally, so your spine is in a natural upright position and your pelvis is neutral. Be careful not to sit too far back in a chair position, this will put you behind the movement of your horse, or too far forward, which tips you onto the forehand and bends your spine unnaturally. Either of these two positions, over time, will cause you back pain, and your horse will also be uncomfortable too.

A couple of good exercises to do when you get on your horse to put you in the deepest part of the saddle, are, firstly, 'legs away'; open your hips and move your upper thighs outwards away from the saddle, then relax; and secondly, grab your thigh muscles from behind and pull them back towards the back of the saddle, this will put you in really close contact with the saddle, and also give you a more effective leg position.

## Seat bone square halt exercise

Feel your seat bones on the saddle.

In walk, feel each seat bone as your horse's legs step underneath. Now halt, and try to feel if one of your horse's hind legs is trailing out behind, or if they feel even, and you have a square halt. If you feel one of your seat bones is dipped down, then this is the side of your horse that his hind leg is trailing behind. You can communicate directly with his hindquarters, by using your leg on the side that is trailing, and give a little squeeze to encourage him to step that leg underneath. He will then step under with this foot.

To practice getting a good square halt, ride forwards into the halt. Pick a letter around the school to aim for, and try to place your body level with that letter. Use your legs and your seat equally into a restricting hand, so you are not losing the energy behind. Once you are in halt, focus on your seat bones, and ask yourself again, is one lower than the other? Practice makes perfect with this.

The trick to getting a good 'square halt', is to ride up into the halt, rather than letting your horse's energy dwindle to a stop. This way, his hind legs will stay engaged and stepping under his body, not trailing behind.

## Sitting Trot

To help keep a long leg and stop them rising up in sitting trot, think of stretching your knee down to the ground.

To be able to sit to the trot your hips need to be loose and flexible. The parts of your body which touch the horse, have to move with him in trot to give the illusion that you are sitting still (and not bouncing about).

Concentrate on feeling your horse's stride swinging, and follow the movement with your seat bones. For a moment, forget about your overall position and concentrate solely on your seat bones, otherwise you will have tension in your body that will block you feeling his stride.

Now, starting in walk, just concentrate on your seat bones, and how they feel, your hips need to be relaxed and flexible. The best way to describe the feeling you are looking for is that your seat bones should be walking in time with your horse's stride, alternate, left then right, you do not need to do anything except let them follow the movement, feel how they 'walk' with the stride of your horse, left seat bone, then right seat bone.

Now, focusing on your seat, just ask your horse for a slow jog trot, do not do anything different with your seat, just allow your seat bones to carry on 'walking' with the stride, it should feel the same, only a bit quicker.

This is a great way to help with learning to sit to the trot, without bouncing out of the saddle. Trust me, you will know when you get it right, it will feel great. If you try this you will be 'plugged in' to your horse, and not a separate entity bouncing about. See how much easier your horse finds moving forward without having to compensate for you bouncing on his back, you will both be smiling, I guarantee.

## Your aids

Generally, your leg aid should be an inward and forward motion. If your aid does not work on first asking, then apply the correct aid again. Don't change the way you are asking your horse, or he will learn incorrectly, you need to be consistent. When you use your aids, as soon as your horse responds stop applying the aid; this is his reward, his thank you.

You need to be on the same team as your horse. If you keep asking your horse, by keep nagging with your aids, with no reward, he will quickly see no point to it, and will disengage with you, and not listen to what you are asking. You want to aim for an equal partnership, of trust and willingness. This is the way to build your relationship and your confidence.

Your rein should be a passive resistance. Your hands should sit in a comfortable regular position, and you should not pull back past this point towards your body. If your horse pulls you, do not pull back, just keep your hands fixed at this point and he will learn that it is comfortable here when he doesn't pull.

**Always remember to reward your horse by 'doing nothing'**

As soon as you get the response you want, relax. This gives your horse a reward, as the biggest reward he can have is you not continually nagging with your legs, hands etc. For example, when you ask him for more forward movement, the second he responds, release your aids. He will then associate his correct response with a reward. This will build a good relationship between you both, and mean that you can keep your aids light, and his response will get quicker. Constant aiding will lead to an unresponsive horse.

**The horse will mirror the rider**

What you want your horse to do, you must do first. He will synchronize with you.

For example; when you want to ride a slower trot, you must slow your rising movement. Don't just keep up with your horse, you need to set the pace you want to go, then he will slow down to your pace. If you just keep up with your horse, the trot will get faster and faster. Stay calm and focused, and in your place; don't let the horse take you, you take the horse.

## Always go back a step

To improve a problem you are having, you need to go back to the previous stage to get an improvement. By keep practising the thing that is going wrong, over and over again, will not improve it. For example; if in your canter transition your horse runs into canter, and is then unbalanced, you need to go back a step and work on the quality of the trot previous to the transition, instead of just repeating the same transition again and again; build a new correct movement in it's place.

Or, you may be stuck in a rut where you horse won't canter, and just runs faster in the trot. The more you try, the more you just keep repeating the cycle of trotting faster. Have you considered that it could be that in your mind you are not 100% committed to the canter transition. Just a small amount of doubt will be transferred through your muscles and body language to your horse.

Remember, horses do not have the same needs as us, and do not have any reason to do a lot of the things we ask of them. Every time you ride you are training your horse; this is why learning to control your emotions around your horse is so important.

## Do you have a 'spooky' area in your school that you like to avoid?

This is a common problem that is encountered a lot. There are some important points to remember; your horse will not associate 'that' corner being spooky. The fact a bird came out on that particular day, or a tractor came around the corner etc, will be completely forgotten by your horse. This is an issue in your mind. Just because that spook happened at that time does not mean it will happen again. It is no more likely to happen in 'that place' than in any other around the school. You ride fine in the other areas. You need to rationalise this in your mind. (As you tense up towards the 'spooky' area, you are giving your horse signals that there is something to be afraid of in that area).

If you have a sensitive horse that tends to be a bit spooky, then staying calm and relaxed is crucial.

When your horse spooks, he will, more often than not, turn his head towards the offending fright, causing his body to swing outwards, this can then be followed by a spin and run.

Firstly, and most important, is to keep a deep seat, stay calm, and centred in the saddle; avoid pulling on the reins, or pulling your knees up, as this will just unbalance you. Keeping your position will enable you to stay with your horse, and not slip out the side door, and you will also be in the best position to bring your horse back to you quickly, and get him under control again.

If you are approaching an area that you know your horse is likely to be spooky, try riding with a slight bend away from the object, so he is bending into the spooky area (practising leg yielding is a good exercise for this). Riding into a spook this way, will help prevent your horse jumping sideways away from the object, and you can then encourage him forwards and successfully past.

As always, keep working on your own body awareness, to improve your balance and security in the saddle, and always practice your breathing as you are riding. Don't be on the look out for a spook; ride confidently forward, and you will minimise the chances of your horse looking for that 'monster'.

Focus on what has gone right in the school and how it has

made you feel, write down your good points after each ride, and use this as your internal dialogue to yourself. Instead of thinking 'what if my horse spooks today' focus on how well you ride. Use your good feelings from your comfort zone to override the negative thoughts that enter your head each time. Keep repeating these positive thoughts to yourself every time you get a negative thought, and your unconscious mind will search for your good feelings, and present these to you instead of the negative emotions. Repetition is the key here. You can do this without being on your horse, all through the day. Its your internal dialogue, to reframe how you think about riding your horse. Gradually you will find you can ride in that 'spooky' corner.

## Transitions will help build your confidence

Variety is key for building confidence during your schooling sessions. Transitions are a great tool for both horse and rider. Remember, every time you ride your horse you are schooling him, be it good or bad! So here are some tips to help improve your transitions:

◆ Performing lots of transitions during your ridden sessions will keep both your's and your horse's mind occupied, which is a great confidence booster, as it gives you something to focus on, instead of the worries going around inside your head. Transitions will improve the communication and bond between you and your horse, ensuring he is tuned into you, and keep his attention on you, preventing him from picking up on distractions.

◆ Keep your schooling sessions short. Your horse can become bored if your sessions are too long, plus you also run the risk of your horse stopping listening to you if it goes on too long. Finish on a good note, and log this in your mind, to build your confidence.

◆ Have purpose and make a plan before each session. Rather than doing long periods of walk and trot around the arena, use shorter bursts. This will keep your horse's mind occupied and ensure he is listening to you. When you trot around the school lacking purpose your horse may switch off and take more interest in his surroundings than in you.

◆　　　　Ride lots of different school figures. Include circles, half circles, demi volts, shallow loops, figure of eights and serpentines. Make it as interesting as possible. Have a play about on some paper beforehand and draw out some figures to try.

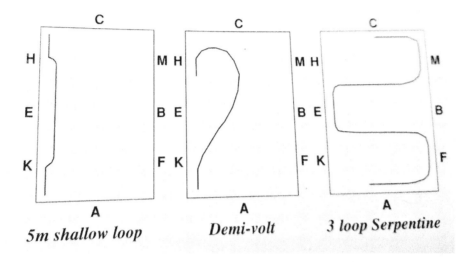

**5m shallow loop**　　　　**Demi-volt**　　　　**3 loop Serpentine**

◆　　　　The half halt should be used before any transitions, this tells your horse that something is going to happen, and rebalances him in readiness. The change from one pace to another should be smooth. The half halt is performed by a leg aid, supple seat and a gentle take and give on the rein, this will collect your horse in preparation for the transition, stopping the energy escaping out the front door, and maintaining his balance.

◆　　　　The quality of the preceding pace will affect the transition. This is very important for confidence, because you want your horse to be balanced, so as you move up and down in the paces you will feel more secure and balanced yourself. For example, if your canter is flat, when you bring your horse forwards to trot, the quality of the trot will also be flat, unbalanced and have an irregular rhythm, causing your horse to run on faster into the trot.

◆       To help you regulate a steady rhythm, try counting along with the stride. For example, in trot, count 1-2, 1-2, 1-2 etc. In canter count 1-2-3, 1-2-3 etc. It is important to keep your counting at a consistent rate, and not speed up if your horse speeds up. By counting out loud in a steady rhythm, it will help you to move at the pace you want, and will help you to keep your horse steady.

◆       Include some direct transitions in your sessions. This is a great way to get  your horse listening to you and using his hind quarters, bringing him off his forehand.  A horse on his forehand is more difficult for the rider to control, and more importantly, for confidence, harder to slow and stop.  Try halt to trot at first. When asking your horse to halt, use the strength in your back and sit deep and tall.  This adjustment alone tells your horse to slow down; use your legs right up to the moment you halt, so you ride forwards into the halt; just restrict your hand movement to halt your horse.  This encourages your horse to halt with his hocks underneath him, and not trailing behind.  This is important with direct transitions, as it will be much easier to take off into trot. Use quick, sharp leg aids and keep a non restraining rein, and ask your horse to go straight into trot.  Encourage him with your voice if it helps.

## Progressing to canter

Problems with the canter transition are one of the commonest. It is often a huge step for a nervous rider to canter, and lots of preparation for this stage will pay dividends for building your confidence. Rushing a canter transition, and being unprepared can shake your confidence. Only progress to canter when you have a good, secure, independent position. Don't feel under pressure to advance too soon, take small steps at a time.

◆       The Canter has a three time beat, with the outside hind leg striking off first, then the diagonal pair move together, and lastly, the 'leading leg' is the inside fore, so called as it stretches further forward (the canter strike off is actually the outside hind leg), followed by a moment of suspension between strides.

◆ For a good quality canter transition make sure you have established a good quality trot prior to asking for canter.

◆ Make sure your position is balanced and upright.

◆ Keep your eyes up, looking ahead, and not down at your horse (he will find it harder to strike off into the canter if you are looking down, as it will put you both off balance).

◆ Do some work on your horses bend, having a good bend will make it easier for your horse to perform a correct canter transition.

◆ Make sure you clearly understand the aids to canter, so you are asking your horse correctly. Your canter aids need to be correct, clear and consistent. As you transition to the canter, have a good, relaxed sitting trot, and place slightly more weight onto your inside seat bone, have your inside leg on the girth, and your outside leg slightly behind (it is your outside leg that asks your horse's outside hind leg to strike off into the canter). Your reins will balance the transition, having an elastic, allowing outside hand, and a soft, allowing inside hand signalling the direction.

◆ Try riding a circle before you canter, and ask for the transition as you come out of the circle up the long side of the arena. This will both help with your horse's bend, and also keep him in a steady rhythm.

◆ Once you are successfully into the canter, relax your seat and allow it to move with your horse, enjoy this pace, it can be much more inviting than the trot, and it is often commented how it is more comfortable.

◆ When asking for your downward transition forwards

to trot, use the same principles as you used for preparation of the upward transition. Ensure your horse is balanced and steady in the canter, balance him with your half halt before asking for the downward transition. Make sure you ride forwards into the trot and steady into a regular rhythm immediately using your position. You want him to still be engaged through the transition, and not lose energy; this will keep him in balance. Loss of balance in your horse does not only happen when he rushes fast, it will also happen if he falls back into trot. So, do not fear the pace, because if you pull on your reins and he falls into the trot, the transition will be too abrupt, and this will unbalance you.

The canter is a lovely, enjoyable pace, and should not be feared. Keep practicing with the tempo and rhythm of your trot and canter paces. Don't expect to be perfect overnight, and don't be disheartened if it does not go to plan. This is completely normal and to be expected, riding takes many hours of practice and repetition, just enjoy the journey, there is no rush. If you have prepared well, then it will be a great experience, and with practice you will soon be looking forward to cantering.

## Hacking

Hacking can be one of the most enjoyable pursuits with your horse, it can be fun and relaxing for both horse and rider.

Rider's are often more comfortable and confident when riding in the confines of the school. Hacking out may fill you with dread. This is understandable because you are venturing outside of your comfort zone, and there are a lot more distractions and hazards.

If you are nervous of hacking there are things you can do to build up your confidence.

Before you venture out hacking with your own horse, arrange to hack out on a bombproof, quiet horse. Maybe book up at a riding school, explaining that you would like to build up your confidence hacking out. An experienced instructor will accompany you, and on these quiet horses you can work on yourself enjoying the experience. You can practice your riding skills in a relaxed manner, using the mental techniques you have learned. As you navigate obstacles and hazards, the instructor can help with your reactions, and to encourage you to relax, so you can practice keeping a relaxed seat and rein, therefore building your body language and communication on this horse, in preparation for hacking out on your own horse. You will soon build up confidence in this situation, and you will be well prepared for communicating your relaxed, confident state to your horse.

You should be using all the mental training techniques you have learned, and also using your new experiences, to log happy memories of hacking into your unconscious mind; replacing any older fears you had.

When you do approach hacking your own horse, make sure you put in place all safety precautions. Wear a body protector, both you and your horse should wear high viz. Take your mobile phone with you (on silent), install 'what3words', which is a great app that will identify your location down to 3 metres, should you get into any problems. Fitting a neck strap on your horse can also be reassuring.

Take a friend with you on the ground, (or your instructor), to walk with you. Stay in walk until you are feeling confident, and build up the distance. At first just go to the end of the lane, or hack around your own yard grounds. If you see hazards up ahead, keep your body language, breathing and rein contact consistent, so you are not changing the communication with your horse, so he knows there is nothing different happening, keep calm and trust in your own ability. You will soon see the benefits of your confidence, as your horse will feed from you and be relaxed too. It is normally best to stay on your horse, however, in some rare instances it can be necessary to dismount and lead your horse past something, but this is really a last resort. If your horse is genuinely scared of something and it is not safe for you to stay on board, do not feel ashamed to dismount and lead him past, to build his confidence that way.

You can build up to walking out with another horse, as long as the companion horse is quiet and experienced, and over time you will be able to introduce trotting and even cantering. Take small steps towards this, so when you are ready to up the pace, make it in small, controlled bursts, that you can easily control. Each good experience will build your confidence.

# CHAPTER 11: UNDERSTANDING YOUR HORSE

Whatever your level of horsemanship, if you have a basic understanding of horse psychology, then it will really help to build your relationship and trust with your horse. You will better understand his needs and behaviour, and you will be able to work with your horse's natural instincts, and not against them. In everyday situations, a knowledge of these instincts is very useful to understanding why he may react in a certain way. By thinking as your horse thinks, you can overcome problems and find solutions, and you will find that as your knowledge grows, so too will your confidence.

Horses have the intelligence of the prey animal, which is very different to our own, as we are predators. This is why horse's are easily startled. As prey animals they naturally use defense mechanisms (instead of reason, as we do), which include flight, speed, shying, rearing and bucking.

Horses are sociable herd animals. In the wild, horse's live in groups; the stallion will lead the group and look out for the mares and youngsters, followed by a dominant mare. Within the group will be smaller herds with a pecking order. Youngsters will play together and develop friendships with mutual grooming (enabling the horse to scratch each other where they cannot reach themselves). Horses also enjoy rolling.

Horse's do not like to be out of sight from other horse's that they know well and are close to. It can be difficult to keep up these social interactions in domesticated settings, and horse's can become isolated. Some yards now keep horse's living together in large barns to try to alleviate these issues.

Horse's have a very strong instinct to cooperate and form friendships. This is great for us, and is why our relationship with our horse's must be based on cooperation and trust, not through fear. A horse will want to please you and be accepted. This is really important to remember in your everyday interactions with your horse, and when training him.

The horse's first instinct is to survive and reproduce. In the wild they were preyed upon and would use speed to survive, running away from danger. The herd always stay together, and if one mare flees, the rest will follow (there is safety in numbers, a horse left alone is easy prey). This natural instinct is still here today, which is why your horse will try to escape from anything unfamiliar that he may perceive as a danger. You have to accept this; your horse cannot reason as you do.

Horses are trickle feeders, and spend over half their time eating and walking, so their stomachs are never completely full, to prevent pressure on their lungs, enabling them to take flight at any time.

They can sleep standing up, and within the herd they will rest at different times, so there is always a lookout for possible predators. They use their sight and hearing senses. Horse's have all round vision, except for a small blind spot directly in front and behind. This is why you should always approach your horse at an angle, towards his shoulder, so you do not startle him. Each ear has numerous muscles which give them mobility and good all round hearing. Because they have such good hearing they can easily recognise different words and tones, which you can use to your advantage in training your horse.

If the horse can't run away from danger, it will defend itself, it may spin and kick out, lunge with it's teeth or strike out with it's front legs. You may have witnessed a stabled horse exhibiting some of these behavoiurs if they feel scared or threatened. This is why you must handle your horse in a kind, calm and confident manner.

## Your domesticated horse

Your horse still needs to feel part of a herd, and will rarely like to be alone.

He will enjoy wandering around the field, grazing. Your horse's stomach is relatively small, which is why we feed them small meals. The use of hay in between meals helps to imitate natural feeding patterns.

Horse's have very good memories and learn by association. A memory of pain can be difficult to remove. Pleasant associations can be formed by rewarding your horse when he shows the behaviour you would like, thereby making it more readily repeated in the future. Horse's are very sensitive to good treatment, praise and reproaches.

In domesticated settings, it is usual on yards for stallions to be kept separate from mares and geldings, as it would be natural for the stallion to try to mate with the mares and fight with the geldings.

Mare and geldings can happily share the same field, although sometimes there can be arguments over dominance, and there will be a specific pecking order within the group. On some yards mares and geldings are kept separately.

## Horse Behaviour

To be happy, your horse needs to be allowed to be a horse. Behaviour issues are more common in horse's that cannot fulfil their natural needs.

It is important to be aware of your horse's usual behaviour patterns. As a horse owner, you will be familiar with your horse's personality, and just like people, horse's have their own personalities and behaviour traits. They may be naturally grumpy, nervous, or laid back.

Never dismiss any new or different behaviours in your horse, as these could be an alarm bell. There could be a logical explanation for the change, or it could be that you can't identify a cause; in which case it should be investigated. If your horse is clearly upset by something, give him the time to find out why. Take a step back and listen to what your horse is trying to tell you.

Maybe your horse normally stands quite while you put his saddle on and do up his girth, and then, for no obvious reason, he starts to object to this; it could be a sign that he is in pain.

Be alert to anything 'out of the ordinary' when you are riding your horse. Unless your horse is obviously lame, recognising when your horse is in pain can sometimes be difficult to feel. Stay observant to abnormal movement, weight distribution, hollowing of the back, stretching or twisting of the neck, or throwing his head up high, as these could all be signs that your horse is in pain.

Horses will normally try to run away or escape from pain. Bucking, rushing forwards, or refusing to move can all be warning signs. Head carriage differences, such as twisting of head, or head shaking, can be early signs of dental problems.

Undesirable behaviours may not just be because your horse is in pain; over exuberance, anxiety, or just stubbornness, can all be reasons for behavioural issues. Remember, horses can have 'off days' too, just like us. Hopefully, as you know your horse best, you will be able to tell the difference.

Boredom can lead to issues in ridden work, so keep schooling sessions varied and interesting.

## Tips to keep your horse happy:

• Learn as much as you can about what your horse needs to be happy and content. Invest the time in researching good horse management.

• Be kind; never treat a horse harshly, as this can lead to aggressive behaviour.

• Keep a regular routine, horses enjoy the stability of a routine.

• Feed your horse the correct amount for his workload, and include plenty of roughage. You should try to imitate the horse's natural feeding patterns, with a trickle supply of hay. Long periods without feed, can lead to vices such as crib biting and wind sucking.

• Horses are gregarious and need other equine contact and interaction. Without this, they will become bored and lonely. Try to ensure your horse can see other horses from his stable.

• Try to make your horse's environment as stimulating as possible. Within the stable you could include stable mirrors, a salt lick, and maybe a toy such as a puzzle they have to move about to release treats, such as carrots. If a horse is just expected to stand around in his stable for hours on end, with nothing to stimulate him, he can easily become bored, which will lead to behavioural issues.

• Give your horse enough turnout time. Your horse should spend a lot of his day walking about, grazing, to emulate natural patterns. Limited turnout and stabling for long periods, can lead to stable vices, such as box walking and weaving.

• Practice good husbandry, ensure good management by giving him regular dental checks, regular foot maintenance, vaccinations, and worming.

• When training your horse, you must take into account how

he learns. If you are not considerate to your horse in his training, then he may exhibit behavioural issues that are not related to pain, but related to him being unhappy. Make sure the fault is not with your communication. You need to be clear and consistent in your training, so as not to confuse your horse. He will usually try to cooperate, but if your signals are not clear, his response will be unclear too, and may not be what you were expecting.

• Remember not all horses are suited to all disciplines. Find out what your horse is best at, and what he enjoys most. Then together you can nurture both your attributes.

• Make sure you give your horse 'days off'. An over worked horse is not a happy horse.

• Check your equipment and tack regularly, to make sure these are still in good working order, and do not cause any soreness to your horse.

Vices are usually a sign that the horse does not have all his natural needs met, and you should try to resolve these issues, for the benefit of you both. When you understand your horse's natural lifestyle and instincts, you can better understand where problems might stem from.

## Body language

Horse's are very good at expressing how they are feeling through their body language. If you observe horse's in different situations, then you can easily learn to read their body language.

When your horse is nervous or scared, his eyes will be wide open looking towards the cause of his anxiety, and his ears will be pricked in the same direction. His nostrils will be flared and blowing, his breathing may be rapid, his muscles will be tense, and he may shake or sweat. You may also notice him leaning back, and even going up on his hind legs.

If your horse is angry, his head will lower and point forwards, his ears will be pinned flat back, and his eyes will appear smaller and look mean, his lips will be taut and he may be showing his teeth. He will also swish his tail.

When your horse is excited, he will hold his head and his tail high, his eyes will be bright, his nostrils flared and blowing and his ears pricked. He may prance about and begin to sweat.

When your horse is relaxed, his lip will appear longer and he will have a relaxed mouth. His ears will move gently about, or may settle outwards. His body will be without tension.

If your horse is submissive towards you, his head will be pointed out, his ears sideways, and his eyes will be half closed. He will be

mouthing (where his lips will snap together), and his muscles will be relaxed.

## Horse vocals

Obviously horse's can't talk, but they do have a vocal language. A friendly nicker is something you will hear from your horse when he is pleased to see you. This is one of the most pleasurable sounds to hear from your horse. He might let you know he is there around feeding time, with a loud neigh or whinny. The horse's neigh can be long and loud, and has different tones. It can be a call for attention. Often a high pitched neigh can be heard when your horse is separated from friends.

If your horse sighs, it could mean he is relaxed or bored, he will exhale outwards with a small sound.

Your horse can express discomfort by groaning; if he also has his ears back and looks angry, he may be in pain. If this happens you should investigate, as he may be in some discomfort.

Snorting and blowing can happen after exercise, or when your horse is excited or stressed.

If you have a mare you may be familiar with the squeel, often asserting their dominance to other horses, or a defensive sound telling others to get out of their space.

A roar from a horse is only really heard when horses are seriously fighting, often heard from stallions in the wild.

## Equine behaviour characteristics:

- Horse's are very active animals, both physically and mentally.
- They are a flight animal and can move and change direction at speed.
- Horse's only sleep for around 2-3 hours in 24 hours.
- Horse's are all individual.
- They have an incredibly good memory.

- A pronounced herd instinct.
- A highly developed sense of direction.
- A dependence on habit.
- An extremely discerning sense of smell.
- Sensitive to noise and other external stimuli.
- Horse's have very sensitive skin (you may have witnessed this when you see a fly landing on your horse, and he twitches it away).
- Very sensitive to good treatment, praise and reproaches.
- Very good at expressing their feelings through expression.
- They can be unpredictable.
- Horse's have a language of their own.
- Horse's are not born vicious, but they can develop this behaviour through poor management.

To keep your horse happy, it is important to take into consideration all of their natural instincts. Still to this day their instincts are very present. The modern methods of keeping horses can be restrictive, compared to their natural lifestyle they were designed to live. If you ignore their instincts, it can lead to behavioural issues. Try to let a horse be a horse as much as possible in domestication, and avoid stress by having thoughtful management.

We must not forget what a privilege it is to be able to spend time with, and enjoy the company of horses, and should not take this for granted. Throughout history they have been our constant companions, without malice. The horse is a gracious animal, so strong, yet so gentle. Horses are wonderful animals to be around, they heal us both inside and out. You only need to look at the therapeutic evidence to see how extraordinary they are. We are incredibly lucky they allow us to share their companionship so willingly.

# CONCLUSION

Horse riding confidence is not something you can just 'magic up', it can take time to build true, long lasting confidence, and here in this book you have been introduced to a formula to build your confidence from within. Correct solid foundations, gaining as much knowledge as you can, and taking small steps, are all key to building your confidence with your horse.

Mindset training is an invaluable tool to have, and is now widely considered to be as important as practical training. Having an understanding of how your fears can grow inside your head, and may spiral out of control, will help you to recognise and overcome these situations. With your mindset training, you can now turn around these thoughts, and bring them under control.

Equipped with the mental and physical training methods, you will soon be on your way to achieving your dreams.

You can act right now; you have the skills you need to begin your exciting journey to confidence with your horse.

# ABOUT THE AUTHOR

## Emma Cooper

Emma is a freelance horse riding coach, who helps nervous and novice riders to overcome their fears and achieve their dreams.

Emma's love for horses started at a young age, having grown up around horses. This passion led her to follow her dream of working with horses, and Emma has been lucky enough to work at a variety of different yards, from starting out as a working pupil on an Arabian Stud, to the position of Senior Instructor at a large Riding Centre, and many places in between!

She worked her way up the qualifications ladder, becoming a qualified Horse Riding Instructor in 1999, and then went on to achieve a Higher National Certificate in Equine Studies in 2005. Emma also holds a Diploma in Advanced Sports Psychology.

*'Bowler' - A truly gentle soul.*

Printed in Great Britain
by Amazon